BARNES & NOBLE HEALTH BASICS

Fibromyalgia

By Janet Mazur

BARNES
& NOBLE
BOOKS
NEW YORK

About the Author

Janet Mazur is a freelance writer who writes frequently on health issues. She has covered such topics as osteoporosis, Alzheimer's disease, migraines, incontinence, and children's health issues. Her work has appeared in *Parents* and *American Baby,* among other publications. She is a member of the American Society of Journalists and Authors and lives at the New Jersey shore, where she also teaches feature writing to adults.

About the Contributors

Portions of this work were reviewed by Stephen Possick, M.D., Lisa Gale Suter, M.D., and Dennis Turk, Ph.D. The information about some of the complementary therapies was written by Melanie Hulse. The information on meditation and biofeedback was written by Lawrence Edwards, Ph.D.

Barbara J. Morgan Publisher
Barnes & Noble Basics

Barb Chintz Editorial Director
Barbara Rietschel Art Director
Clellen Bryant Editor
Emily Seese Editorial Assistant
Della R. Mancuso Production Manager

Cover Design by **Leonard Vigliarolo**
Illustrations by **Cynthia Saniewski**

Table of Contents

Foreword

Your body aches, you feel exhausted, the slightest effort overwhelms you. What is going on? These symptoms are but a few of the signs of a difficult pain disorder known as fibromyalgia syndrome. Since it first entered the medical lexicon in 1990, doctors have been struggling to define, treat and cure this mysterious disorder. While research is underway, there is much you can do right now to feel better. Inside Barnes & Noble Health Basics *Fibromyalgia,* you'll find expert guidance from leading physicians who can help you understand your symptoms and the various treatments for them.

You'll find useful information on diet and nutrition, complementary therapies, how best to search the Internet and how to put your health care team together. You'll also get the latest news on cutting-edge research and some wise advice on the role of stress and comfort in managing your health.

With all of these helpful insights at your fingertips, you'll be able to take control of your fibromyalgia and become an advocate for your own health care. Remember: An informed patient is an empowered one. So read on to put yourself in the driver's seat when it comes to treating and managing your fibromyalgia.

Barb Chintz
Editorial Director
Barnes & Noble Health Basics Series

CHAPTER 1

Symptoms

Experiencing the symptoms
what's going on?

At first, you pass off the muscle aches and exhaustion as simply more evidence of the stress and strain of your life. Between work and family, cell phones and e-mails, you are wiped out from constant multitasking. Who wouldn't be tired and achy, you ask? Except the exhaustion isn't going away, despite the fact that you're trying hard to get a good night's sleep. And maybe that's also part of the problem—you're sleeping very fitfully, tossing and turning most of the night. If you do manage to sleep, you wake up feeling lousy and your muscles ache. Some days it feels as though you have the flu. You wonder if that is why your stomach acts up and your memory is cloudy. The problem is that this flu doesn't seem to get better. At some point, you visit your primary care doctor to find out what is going on.

If this was your story, then, hopefully, your doctor listened carefully to your concerns and ordered the appropriate screening tests (see pages 12–13). But when the tests came back negative for any underlying cause, such as infection or inflammation, your doctor may have chalked up your complaints to stress and prescribed lifestyle changes, such as exercise and stress reduction, and a follow-up visit in a few months. In addition, your doctor may have suggested a trial of antidepressant therapy (see pages 52–53).

There are several reasons for a misdiagnosis. For starters, you look fine—there is no fever, no pallid skin tone, swollen joints, or other visual symptoms. Also, your symptoms of pain can be hard to describe accurately. (For more on how to overcome this common communication problem, see page 103.) Another reason for a misdiagnosis is lack of knowledge. A lot of primary care doctors are not experienced with the subtleties of complex pain disorders such as **fibromyalgia.** (This disorder didn't enter the medical lexicon until 1990, when a group of doctors officially defined the criteria for the diagnosis.) For all these reasons, it is not surprising that it takes an average of five years before most people get a diagnosis of fibromyalgia.

So what are the symptoms that can arise with fibromyalgia? Most people who have this disorder are stunned at how varied the symptoms can be. They are also amazed at how they can range in severity. In some cases, these symptoms can come on slowly; in others, they come on rapidly following a traumatic event, such as an being in an automobile accident. Having several of these symptoms does not mean that you have fibromyalgia, but it does mean that you need to find a doctor who is familiar with this particular array of symptoms.

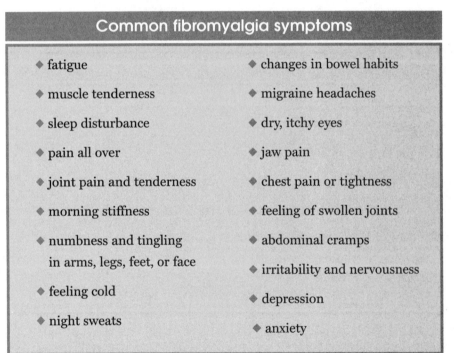

Common fibromyalgia symptoms

- fatigue
- muscle tenderness
- sleep disturbance
- pain all over
- joint pain and tenderness
- morning stiffness
- numbness and tingling in arms, legs, feet, or face
- feeling cold
- night sweats

- changes in bowel habits
- migraine headaches
- dry, itchy eyes
- jaw pain
- chest pain or tightness
- feeling of swollen joints
- abdominal cramps
- irritability and nervousness
- depression
- anxiety

Your emotional symptoms
fibromyalgia can affect your emotional well-being

You may have experienced psychological symptoms as well as physical ones, the most prevalent being depression and anxiety. This makes sense when you realize that chronic pain (pain that lasts longer than six months) can be very debilitating both physically and emotionally. However, depression can lead to many of the symptoms of fibromyalgia and is far more prevalent than fibromyalgia. That's why many doctors will think of depression first, before they consider fibromyalgia. But, in some cases, there can be a dual diagnosis of depression and fibromyalgia.

Emotional Symptoms of Fibromyalgia	
Noticeable anxiety and excitability	Inability to concentrate
Mood swings, including bouts of crying	Loss of interest in normal activities
Irritability and impatience	Confused thinking
Impaired memory	Depression
Slowing of mental processes (known as "fibrofog")	Loss of interest in sex
	Withdrawal from friends and family

ASK THE EXPERTS

Why does fibromyalgia affect so many parts of my body, not to mention my moods?

Fibromyalgia is considered a **systemic** pain condition, which means that the symptoms are often found throughout your body. This explains why one day you may have sharp pain in the back of your neck and in your shoulders, and the next day you'll have a killer headache. Another time, you may find yourself depressed for no obvious reason. Mood changes are a part of the condition, too.

It upsets me that some people tell me I look fine, so how can I be so sick?

This is one of the crueler ironies of having fibromyalgia. You don't have any visible symptoms, you just feel awful all the time. This sets you apart from the vast majority of ill or disabled people who usually have some visible "proof" of their ailment. You have only your feeling of pain and fatigue. Because there is nothing to see, a lot of people are dismissive of fibromyalgia. For more on communicating effectively with friends, family, and colleagues, see page 182.

Testing for fibromyalgia
blood tests and X-rays

What types of tests do doctors typically order when a patient comes in complaining of muscle pain and generalized fatigue? Most doctors will order tests that are designed to reveal, among other things, an infection, a hormonal imbalance, an autoimmune problem, and/or inflammation.

The following are blood tests that can help a doctor form a diagnosis:
Complete blood count, or CBC. This inexpensive test measures the red- and white-blood-cell count. An elevated white-blood-cell count can mean an infection, while a low red-blood-cell count can mean several things, such as anemia, which can cause fatigue.

Antinuclear antibody, or ANA. A positive ANA can mean that the blood contains an antibody that is reacting to the body's own nuclear material. Because this test is fairly nonspecific, further testing is needed.

C-reactive protein, or CRP. This nonspecific test reveals the presence of CRP, an abnormal protein produced by the liver during an acute inflammatory flare-up. An elevated CRP requires further testing before a diagnosis of an inflammatory illness can be made.

Creatine phosphokinase, or CPK. This test measures serum levels of CPK, which are found in the the heart muscle, the skeletal muscles, and the brain. Elevated levels can mean muscle damage; however, high levels can happen following a good workout or a heart attack, or in conditions like myositis.

Epstein-Barr virus titer. Epstein-Barr is a virus that infects about 80 percent of the population. Like chicken pox, this virus is carried in the body for life. For the most part it remains dormant, but it can reactivate at various times. Because the body creates antibodies to fight Epstein-Barr virus, the presence of these antibodies can indicate current or prior infection.

Erythrocyte sedimentation rate, or ESR. This nonspecific test, also known as the "sed rate" test, measures the rate at which red blood corpuscles settle in a saline solution over a period of time. Inflammation and infections increase the weight of red blood cells, causing them to descend faster than normal. An elevated sed rate indicates the presence of an inflammatory process, such as rheumatoid arthritis, but further testing is needed.

HLA-B27 antigen test. This test reveals the presence of any HLA antigens. If any of these antigens are found this indicates the likelihood of an inflammatory disease such as rheumatoid arthritis.

Lyme test. A Lyme test may reveal the presence of IgG or IgM antibodies that one's body makes to fight Lyme disease. If these antibodies are found in the blood, it is evidence of current or past Lyme disease.

Thyroid function tests. These blood tests measure the amount of thyroid-stimulating hormones, otherwise known as T_3 and T_4. Low or high levels of these hormones indicate a thyroid disorder, such as hypothyroidism or hyperthyroidism.

Body imaging tests:

Bone X-rays. X-rays of bones are sometimes used to rule out a bone fracture or an infection or tumor in the bone.

Magnetic resonance imaging, or MRI. The MRI is an amazing diagnostic tool that can reveal a host of problems in bones, organs, joints, and soft tissues. Among other things, an MRI can detect herniated spinal disks, lesions of the bone and soft tissue, malignancies, and joint disorders.

Computed tomography, or CT. Like the MRI, the CT is used to image bones and soft tissue.

Nerve conduction testing/electromyelography. These tests are used to test nerve function and can be used to diagnose carpal tunnel syndrome.

Similarities to other illnesses
ruling out other conditions

As your doctor reviews your symptoms and looks at your test results, he or she can begin to line up the possible disorders and diseases that match your symptoms. He or she will then start eliminating those disorders and diseases one by one, until settling on the illness that most likely explains your symptoms.

A few other diseases and conditions have similar symptoms:

Rheumatoid arthritis (also known as RA) is a systemic inflammatory disease that can affect the entire body. It involves inflammation in the lining of the joints and/or other internal organs, which creates pain, stiffness, warmth, redness, and swelling. (Note: The sources of pain in people with fibromyalgia are generally the tendons or ligaments that attach to the muscles, not the joints, as is the case with RA.) Early in the onset of RA, people may feel a general fatigue, soreness, stiffness, and aching. Pain and swelling may occur in the same joints on both sides of the body and will usually start in the hands or the feet. RA can be diagnosed not only by its symptoms and physical findings upon examination, but also by X-rays and a blood test. In the U.S., an estimated 1.5 million women and 600,000 men have RA.

Systemic lupus erythematosus (or lupus) is a chronic autoimmune inflammatory disorder of the connective tissue that can affect various body parts, especially the joints and skin, as well as the internal organs. The symptoms can include swelling and pain in the joints, muscle pain and weakness, fatigue, skin lesions, hair loss, fever, and headaches. Lupus can be diagnosed by blood tests. For many people, lupus is a mild disease affecting only a few organs. For others, it can cause serious and life-threatening problems. More than 16,000 people develop it each year, and it is estimated that 500,000 to 1.5 million Americans have been diagnosed with lupus.

Lyme disease is an acute inflammatory disease caused by a tick-borne organism called a spirochete. It can cause swollen joints, fatigue, fever, chills, and headache. A diagnosis can be made by a blood test for Lyme as well as the presence of a skin rash surrounding the tick-bitten area. A course of antibiotics will usually eradicate the disease if begun early.

Hypothyroidism is an illness in which the amount of thyroid hormone in the body is below normal, resulting in a lowered metabolic rate and a general loss of vigor. Hypothyroidism is the most common thyroid abnormality. Symptoms include feeling run-down, intolerant to cold, depressed, and disinterested in daily activities. Other symptoms include dry and brittle hair, dry and itchy skin, constipation, muscle cramps, and, in women, increased menstrual flow. Treatment involves taking daily thyroid hormone supplements.

ASK THE EXPERTS

One of my tests results showed that I had lupus, but it turned out to be a false positive. What is a false positive and how can that happen?

A **false positive** is when you test positive for a condition you don't have. It happens for a number of reasons. Sometimes it is a simple laboratory error, and for that reason doctors often order the test again if a positive result comes back pointing to a serious disorder. Also, illness markers, such as a herniated disk in an MRI or the ANA antibody for lupus, are present in healthy people as well as sick people. Approximately half the population have one or more disk problems but don't have any back pain. A small percentage, about five percent, of healthy people will test positive for the ANA antibody that reveals lupus, but they do not have the disease. That's why one test result should not be used as the basis for a diagnosis. Ideally, the same test should be taken again and other tests should be given to confirm a diagnosis.

Getting a diagnosis
it can take longer than you think

You have been given numerous diagnostic tests and they have all come back negative. In other words, there is no underlying physical pathology that can be identified as the cause of your symptoms. Depending on your doctor, you may be sent on your way and told to take it easy. For most people with fibromyalgia, this is their story. In fact, the average time between the onset of symptoms and a proper diagnosis of fibromyalgia syndrome is five years. But if you are lucky, you have a doctor who knows something about a pain syndrome known as fibromyalgia and how to test for it.

While there is no definitive blood test for fibromyalgia syndrome, there is a specific pain pattern and symptom pattern that can point to a diagnosis. The word syndrome means a collection of symptoms that appear to occur in the absence of an identified cause. As of 1990 when fibromyalgia syndrome was officially included in the list of rheumatological disorders, there is a very simple diagnostic test that can confirm the illness. In fibromyalgia the soft tissues of the neck, shoulders, chest, and buttocks are especially tender and can develop **tender points**—specific areas that cause pain when pressed. In 1990, a set of 18 tender points was created.

FIRST PERSON INSIGHTS

Finally it has a name

I nearly gave up. After more than a year of describing my symptoms—pain, severe exhaustion, and muscle aches—to several doctors and getting no satisfaction, I began to think I was crazy. Maybe it *was* all in my head. After all, the symptoms did come and go. Eventually, with a bit of luck and loads of encouragement from my grown daughter, I found a sympathetic rheumatologist. He listened to my symptoms and pressed various spots on my body and gave me a diagnosis: fibromyalgia. All the pieces finally seemed to fit together, and in some ways, I felt so relieved. At least I know it's not all in my head.

—Brenda P., Lansing, MI

Fibromyalgia Tender Points

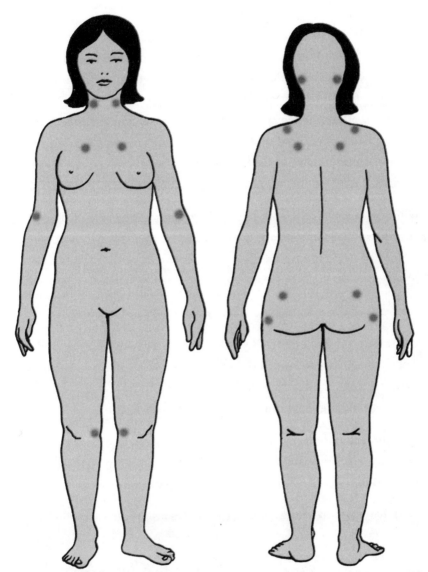

To test for fibromyalgia a doctor presses firmly on each of these 18 tender points. For a diagnosis of fibromyalgia, a person needs to feel pain in at least 11 out of the 18 tender points and these points need to be distributed above and below the waist, as well as on either side of the body and along the spine. In other words, the tender points cannot be concentrated in just one or two areas of the body. Moreover, the pain must have been felt for at least three months and have no known explanation, such as injury or infection.

Why me, why now?
there are a number of reasons

Fibromyalgia is a syndrome marked predominantly by chronic muscle pain and sleep disturbances that has no identified organic cause, such as an infection or virus. This does not mean it is a psychosomatic disease—one of those unexplained disorders that medical science has historically blamed on personality flaws. Not very long ago, ulcers were thought to be caused by nerves it wasn't until the 1980s that researchers realized that a vast majority of ulcers are due to bacterial infection and can be easily treated with antibiotics.

While researchers still work to find the cause of fibromyalgia, they have already discovered a number of contributing factors:

- **Physical trauma.** Fibromyalgia often occurs after a physical trauma—an illness or an injury, especially to the neck, such as a car accident—which can act as a trigger in the development of the disorder.

- **Interrupted sleep cycles.** One of the big issues with fibromyalgia is poor sleep. Researchers have found that those with fibromyalgia have trouble maintaining deep sleep, or stage four of the sleep cycle. It is during this stage that muscles and tissues are repaired.

- **Hormonal imbalances.** Researchers have noted that people with fibromyalgia have abnormal levels of growth hormone and the stress hormone, cortisol. (For more on this, see page 158.)

- **Environmental issues.** Some researchers are wondering whether exposure to certain chemicals in the environment might trigger or worsen the symptoms of fibromyalgia.

◆ **Central-nervous-system problems.** Recent studies suggest that people with fibromyalgia have a generalized disturbance in the way their central nervous system processes pain. Pain perception is regulated by the brain via neurotransmitters (chemicals that transmit information within the brain). One of the pain neurotransmitters, called substance P, is elevated threefold in the spinal fluid of people with fibromyalgia. Thus, any type of movement or exercise is perceived as painful. For more on pain amplification, see page 32.

◆ **Genetics.** You may have inherited a gene that predisposes you toward fibromyalgia. Often the illness is seen in families, among siblings or mothers and their children. According to some studies, 10 percent of people with fibromyalgia have a relative who either has or had it.

◆ **Sexual abuse.** There is a prevalence of sexual and physical abuse in women with fibromyalgia syndrome. Some people with fibromyalgia who were sexually abused as children wonder whether memories of the abuse, no matter how long ago it took place, are stored in the body, triggering the onset of the disorder. Researchers continue to explore this possibility.

The bigger picture
you are not alone

It's been confirmed. You have been given a diagnosis of fibromyalgia, and you're feeling a bit, well, overwhelmed. It may cushion the blow to know that you are far from alone. Many people have it. Estimates run as high as four million people in the U.S., including sitcom star Larry Wilcox (*CHiPs*) and Jennifer Watkins, Miss Pennsylvania USA 2001. If they can have an accomplished life, you can too.

Although a higher percentage of women are impacted, the condition does not discriminate, striking men, women and children of all ages and races. Those who are most likely to develop fibromyalgia:

- Women in their mid-30s to late 50s.

- Men and women age 70 or older.

- People who also have an autoimmune disorder, such as lupus or rheumatoid arthritis.

- Those who have recently had an infectious disease, such as Lyme disease.

- Those who have recently had a traumatic accident or injury.

Is there anything I did to place myself in a higher risk category for the illness?

No. Nothing you consciously did brought on your condition. While fibromyalgia can occur at any age, the chances of getting this disorder increase as you age. Fibromyalgia sometimes occurs with other muscle or joint diseases or chronic pain conditions. This can make the condition terribly difficult to diagnose. For a correct diagnosis to be made, your doctor must first identify the symptoms and then rule out other possible disorders. What makes matters confusing is that fibromyalgia can co-exist with other disorders.

How common is fibromyalgia among children?

In one study, juvenile fibromyalgia was found in 1.2 percent of school-children, all girls. Another study found that it typically developed after age 13. Symptoms are similar to those experienced by adults. (For more on children and fibromyalgia, see pages 73–82.)

Fibromyalgia 911
what you can do right now for relief

The pain of fibromyalgia can be unbearable: "It's like my muscles are on fire." "I feel as if I had been run over by a truck and then got the flu." "If I want to do anything, I need to take a nap afterward." While there are a number of medications and therapies for you and your doctor to consider (see pages 39–62), there are certain simple things you can do right now that will help you get through the day:

- Apply a warm heating pad or air-activated heatwraps to your muscles.

- Do gentle stretches. See pages 56–57.

- Take a hot shower or bath.

- Ask someone to massage a tight muscle, or see if you can schedule a quick massage.

- Steer clear of anything that is increasing your muscle tension—for example, bright sunlight, uncomfortable clothes, loud music, or noise.

- Change your physical position frequently. This is especially important if you are sitting or lying down for long periods. Be sure to get up and move around every half hour or so.

- Try to avoid negative thoughts ("I will never get better!") that will further add to your muscle tension.

- Practice deep breathing. See page 141 for instructions.

- Drink plenty of water and have light, healthy snacks.

Practical tips

Re-adjusting your posture as you go about your daily business can do much to spare you from a fibromyalgia flare-up of pain and can conserve your energy as well. Here are some tips:

In the kitchen

When you are preparing food or washing dishes, place one foot on a footstool and stand up straight, or simply open a cabinet door and place one foot on the ledge to ease the strain on your back.

At work

Make sure your chair has good low-back support and armrests. Lean forward at your hips instead of bending at the waist or neck.

In the car

Sit up straight, and don't lean in close to the steering wheel. Make sure your car's seats are fully adjustable and have armrests and a headrest that you can position to support the middle of your head.

Reading

Instead of lying down in bed or on your side, sit in a firm chair with stable spine support.

Moving Smart

When you lift or carry an object, keep it close to your body. If possible, slide objects across the floor rather than lifting and carrying them. Carry a purse with a shoulder strap, bearing the weight on your larger shoulder joints to ease the stress on elbows, wrists, and fingers. Consider using a waist pack rather than a purse to eliminate stress on your lower back.

Keeping a health journal
learning to listen to your body

One of the best ways to take care of yourself when you are confronted with a chronic illness, such as fibromyalgia, is to learn to pay attention to your body by keeping track of your health in a health journal. By writing down changing symptoms, you will be learning how to really listen to your body and understand what it is trying to tell you. Over time, this health journal will be an invaluable tool that will enable both you and your doctors to recognize patterns that point to the right disorder.

Your health journal will be very helpful to your recovery as well. How so? Treatment for fibromyalgia does not necessarily happen overnight. It sometimes takes time to determine the right combination of exercise, medication and other therapies that can ease your symptoms and improve your physical and emotional functioning. By noting changes in your symptoms as you undergo them, you can plot the success of various treatments. A health journal is a powerful tool that can save you time and unnecessary suffering. It also does a wonderful job of reminding you that you, not your doctors, are in charge of your health.

Sample of a Health Journal

Get a three-ring binder and fill it with loose-leaf paper. Next, set aside a time every week to record how you feel. Keep it simple. Cover each major body system and identify any symptoms. Grade each symptom on a scale of 0 to 10, with 0 being nonexistent and 10 being a major concern. Your goal is to track the lessening or worsening of any symptoms. If you wish, make copies of the chart below and use it to find patterns to your symptoms.

DATE							
SYMPTOMS							
Morning stiffness							
Muscle weakness							
Diarrhea							
Constipation							
Muscle pain							
Fatigue							
Poor appetite							
Ravenousness							
Feelings							
Upbeat							
Depressed							
Low energy							
High energy							
Sleep							
Insomnia							
Excessive sleep							

Helpful resources

The Chronic Illness Workbook;
Strategies and Solutions for Taking
Back Your Life
by Patricia A. Fennell

All About Fibromyalgia; A Guide for
Patients and Their Families
by Daniel J. Wallace, M.D. and
Janice Brock Wallace

Fibromyalgia for Dummies
by Roland Staud with
Christine Ademec

National Institute of Arthritis
and Musculoskeletal and
Skin Diseases
Information Clearinghouse
NIAMS/National Institutes
of Health
1 AMS Circle
Bethesda, MD 20892-3675
301-565-2966
www.niams.nih.gov

Arthritis Foundation
1330 West Peachtree Street
Atlanta, GA 30309
800-283-7800
404-872-7100
www.arthritis.org

Fibro Community
www.fibrohugs.com

CHAPTER 2

Fibromyalgia Explained

A complex disorder
Fibromyalgia syndrome defined

At last there is a name for all that you've been experiencing. So what exactly is it? Fibromyalgia is considered by some to be a form of soft-tissue **rheumatism**. (Rheumatism is any painful condition involving the joints, ligaments, or muscles.) In the case of fibromyalgia, there is widespread pain and tenderness (soreness to the touch) at very specific body sites. It has been noted in medical archives for centuries as a curious muscle disorder that affects men, women, and children. In 1990, a noted rheumatologist named Dr. Frederic Wolfe published a paper that was the first to lay out a clinical understanding of the mysterious disorder, known then as fibrositis, which was considered an inflammation of the muscles. Since biopsies of muscles revealed no inflammation, Dr. Wolfe decided to rename the disorder. Fibromyalgia is made up of both Latin and Greek words. *Fibro* is Latin for the connective tissue of tendons and ligaments, *myo* is Greek for muscle and, *algia* is Greek for pain.

Dr. Wolfe, along with various colleagues, codified the precise symptoms, namely a history of widespread pain in all four quadrants of the body for at least three months. What this means is that the pain shows up on both the right and left sides of your body, as well as above and below your waist and down the spine. For a diagnosis of fibromyalgia there needs to be pain in at least 11 of 18 designated tender points when a specific amount of pressure is applied (see page 17).

Not all of the medical community has agreed with these diagnostic criteria for fibromyalgia. In fact, there are some doctors who feel that it is a psychosomatic syndrome that should never have been given the official medical status of a disease. Until research finds the ultimate cause of fibromyalgia, no one can really know for sure.

If the disorder has been known since 1990, and the disease is so widespread, how come so many doctors know so little about it?

Since people with fibromyalgia usually look healthy and conventional tests typically turn out normal, it takes a savvy and knowledgeable physician to make a correct diagnosis. What makes it even more complicated is that you may be experiencing different symptoms each time you visit the doctor, and sometimes these symptoms will seem totally unrelated! Also, no two people have the same symptoms or experience fibromyalgia in quite the same way. With a condition this multi-faceted, is it any wonder doctors find it maddening, and don't want to leap to an immediate diagnosis?

I'm confused. Is the pain of fibromyalgia in the muscles, joints, or tendons?

The pain is in all three—muscles, joints and tendons.

Is a tender point the same thing as a trigger point?

No, they are different. The tender points of fibromyalgia are the 18 specific spots in the body that register pain in response to pressure—usually about nine pounds, about what it would take to push a thumbtack into a wall. **Trigger points**, on the other hand, can be found anywhere in the muscles of the body. They feel very tight to the touch. Moreover, upon touch the pain is often felt to radiate elsewhere in the body. Trigger points are found in myofacial pain syndrome (see pages 66–67). That said, some people with fibromyalgia can also have trigger points.

The phases of fibro
riding an emotional roller coaster

Fibromyalgia is not a degenerative disorder, nor is it progressive. It does not have distinct phases the way other illnesses do. While some people do happily report that their symptoms diminish over time—usually a few years— some are not so lucky. Does this make fibromyalgia a chronic disorder? To some yes; to others no. What is true is that its symptoms are likely to wax and wane. As one fibromyalgia patient put it, "One step forward, five steps back."

One week, you may feel reasonably fine, if a bit more tired than usual. Another week, you'll find you've overdone it. Whether you've put in extra hours in the office or spent too much time shuttling your children to too many events, you've gone too far. The result is a lost, achy weekend spent in bed, resting and hoping to recover your strength.

Meantime, you are riding an emotional roller coaster. At first you may feel relief at having identified the demon that's been plaguing you and knowing that it is not life-threatening. At other times, you are mad as hell at all the changes you've been forced to make in your lifestyle (see Chapter 11 for helpful coping tips). At the same time, you may notice that people have begun to treat you differently. You may sense disbelief on their part: After all, you don't look sick. Others expect you to snap out of it: How could anyone continue to be sick for so long?

Experts say this is a common reaction for several reasons: Our culture has a difficult time accepting chronic illness. Either you are sick and you get better, or you get progressively sicker and die. Even health care professionals receive little training in the real experience of chronic illness, which follows its own cycle of relapse and recovery.

Chronic Pain

Thanks to a number of medical diseases and conditions, more Americans are in chronic pain than you might think. Some estimates range as high as 50 million. However, according to Dr. Daniel J. Clauw of Georgetown University Medical Center, people with chronic pain also usually have other pain symptoms. In the U.S. population, an estimated:

♦ 10 percent have chronic widespread pain.

♦ 20 percent have chronic regional pain.

♦ 15 percent have severe fatigue.

♦ 15 percent have irritable bowel syndrome.

♦ 10 percent have migraines.

♦ 50 to 60 percent have tension headaches.

Since these symptoms tend to cluster in individuals, there is considerable overlap among systemic conditions, such as fibromyalgia, chronic fatigue syndrome, multiple chemical sensitivity, and Gulf War syndrome, as well as among "organ-specific" diagnoses, such as irritable bowel syndrome, migraine and tension headaches. (Source: "Elusive Syndromes" by Dr. Daniel J. Clauw, *Cleveland Clinic Journal of Medicine*, Oct. 2001).

Pain amplification
when a gentle touch hurts

One of the more mysterious aspects of fibromyalgia is the nature of the pain people feel. Fibromyalgia patients report pain in places where there is no injury or organic problem. Doctors call this **allodynia**. What causes this phenomenon of pain amplification where even the slightest touch can feel painful? Again, there are a number of theories.

Some scientists theorize that people with fibromyalgia process pain differently than those without the condition. When a part of your body is injured or damaged, nerves in that area release various chemical alarm signals, including **substance P**. This neurotransmitter stimulates a host of reactions, such as tensing up to protect the injured area and releasing other neurotransmitters, such as **serotonin**, which regulate the body's ability to cope with the pain. Some experts believe that people with fibromyalgia have elevated levels of substance P, and lower than normal levels of serotonin. Other scientists theorize that it is the repetitive aspect of fibromyalgia pain that causes the problem. Repeated pain stimuli cause some part of the pain system to change, resulting in pain amplification.

Thanks to experiments comparing MRI brain scans of healthy, pain-free people with those of fibromyalgia patients, experts can now see that there is a biological difference in the way people with fibromyalgia process pain. For starters, the memory of pain lasts longer. Dr. Roland Staud of the University of Florida College of Medicine, Gainesville, has done some interesting research into this phenomenon of **pain decay**. In most people, once a pain stimulation stops, the sensation of pain goes away, or decays, in a minute or two. In fibromyalgia patients, the pain decay takes much longer, especially when the pain is caused by heat. Dr. Staud concludes that people with fibromyalgia may have a **central sensitization** to pain; in other words, the memory of pain does not go away.

It's All in Your Chemistry

Substance P

When your body is injured, a neural hormone called substance P is released in the neurons and in the spinal cord. Its purpose is to send a pain message back to the brain. Research has shown that levels of substance P in the spinal cord of fibromyalgia patients can be up to three times higher than in other people.

Serotonin

When you feel something painful, your body has a clever method for turning down the volume on the pain message. Serotonin, a neurotransmitter that regulates the brain's ability to control pain and mood, is a substance that is released in your brain and spinal cord to accomplish this task, diminishing the pain.

Experts have found that serotonin levels may be low or may be poorly processed in those with fibromyalgia. Serotonin also facilitates deep, restful sleep. A lack of it may lead directly to a lack of this deep sleep, a common symptom in fibromyalgia.

The gate theory of pain
you can learn to close the gate

Sometimes, your pain vanishes or reappears for no apparent reason. People with severe injuries may feel nothing at all at first. On the other hand, as anyone who has fibromyalgia can attest, pain can suddenly flare, traveling to uninjured parts of your body. Why does this happen?

Some experts call this the "gate" theory of pain. In a nutshell, this theory proposes that as pain signals travel to and from the brain, they pass through a pain gate that can be opened or closed by various factors. For the most part, the gate opens upon injury and is closed when neurotransmitters such as serotonin and **endorphins** block the pain. Some medicines, such as morphine and other narcotic pain relievers, work by imitating the body's endorphins and blocking the pain signal, thus closing the gate to pain. For that matter, research shows that soothing warm baths, rest, and even quiet meditation can also cause a release of these gate-closing neurotransmitters.

In the case of fibromyalgia, researchers theorize that the gate is somehow stuck in the open position. This would explain the constant sensation of pain and also the fact that traditional pain relievers often don't work as well as they do in people who don't have fibromyalgia.

What opens your gate? If you answer "yes" to any of the questions below, you may need to rethink your pain management plan.

- Are you using up your pain medication faster than you used to?

- Are you spending all day in bed on a regular basis?

- Are you smoking to relax?

- Are you avoiding any kind of exercise?

- Are you drinking alcohol several times a day?

Pain Diary

Pain can feel "like a black hole that consumes everything thing in its path," writes Dr. James Dillard, author of *The Chronic Pain Solution*. To help make sense of it, he suggests you track its course. To that end, Dr. Dillard suggests creating your own pain diary. He says it is best to keep tabs on the pain at the same select times every day. In your diary, note your pain level (on a scale from 1 to 10 with 10 being the most painful, see pages 24–25), what caused the pain (an activity, stress, etc.), and how you responded to it (exercise, medication, etc.), and whether that response helped or hurt. Here is a sample below to use when creating your pain diary.

Date/Time	Level of Pain	Possible Causes	Your Response	Result

Sleep dysfunction
plenty of evidence, but no smoking gun

Serotonin, the neurotransmitter that regulates your body's ability to control pain and mood, also facilitates deep, restorative sleep. Some experts believe that levels of serotonin may be low or poorly processed in fibromyalgia patients. That may be why sleeplessness rates right up there with muscular aches as the most common complaint from people with fibromyalgia.

Compounding matters is the fact that lowered serotonin levels may also lower the secretion of growth hormones in the body. In fact, a 1992 study at Oregon Health Sciences University showed that people with fibromyalgia have much lower levels of **somatomedin**, a peptide that is secreted primarily in the fourth stage of sleep and is essential in the body's task of rebuilding itself. It is during that sleep stage that damaged tissue (including muscle) incurred throughout the day, from normal activities, is repaired. Insufficient levels of growth hormones may mean that damaged cells stay damaged longer, causing pain and other symptoms.

Given these factors, it's easy to understand why deep sleep is so critical and why you feel so rotten when you don't get it! In order to achieve this blissful sleep state, many fibromyalgia patients turn to prescription drugs for help, though so far studies on their effectiveness have been mixed.

Tricyclics, a family of antidepressant drugs that has been around for more than 40 years, can be effective in treating sleep issues because they relax muscles, raise your pain threshold, and promote restorative, **delta-wave sleep**. Tricyclics also increase the amount of serotonin available to your nerve cells and raise the efficiency of endorphins, a hormone needed for regulating pain and for deep sleep. (See pages 52–53 for more on tricyclics.)

Sleep, come free me

I was feeling really happy that I finally found a great doctor who knows a lot about fibromyalgia. He had been really helpful with treating my pain. But getting a good night's sleep proved challenging. He prescribed a drug regimen and was so confident that I'd feel better, he just about guaranteed it. The problem was that it was not working and I felt as though I'd disappointed him. I knew I was being silly, but I felt guilty somehow—as if I had failed him. I finally got up the courage to tell him that the sleeping pills weren't working. He was great about it. In fact, he was surprised I had waited so long to tell him. He said I should never feel guilty about a treatment not working. The problem wasn't me. The problem was that fibromyalgia was very difficult to treat. But he was still confident we would find solutions to my symptoms. He made some really smart suggestions about "sleep hygiene." So now I use my bed only for sleeping, keep to a regular bedtime, have no caffeine after 4 p.m. (that means chocolate, too!) and no alcohol close to bedtime. His suggestions have worked wonders. Better still, our relationship has become more of a partnership than your typical doctor/patient interaction. And that, too, has made a huge difference in how I feel.

—Beth C., Daytona Beach, FL

Helpful resources

*The Arthritis Foundation's Guide to
Good Living with Fibromyalgia*

The Chronic Pain Solution
by Dr. James N. Dillard

*Handbook for Fibromyalgia and
Chronic Muscle Pain*
by Gayle Backstrom and
Bernard R. Rubin

Fibromyalgia
by Dr. Don Goldenberg

CHAPTER 3

Treatments for Fibromyalgia

Your pain management plan
you can create one yourself

There is no single be-all and end-all treatment for fibromyalgia. In fact, the Food and Drug Administration has yet to approve a single treatment specifically aimed at treating the syndrome. However, there are a myriad of options you and your doctor can choose from. Many experts agree that the most effective tack is to combine several different approaches. After all, people with fibromyalgia have many different symptoms, from pain to sleeplessness to fatigue. Why not attack all of them? Your choices range from simple lifestyle changes to over-the-counter pain relievers to aerobic exercise to localized injections for pain. How well they will work will depend in large part on the severity of your case and on you as an individual.

As you start on your journey toward health and well-being, it's a good idea to plot your path. If you haven't done so already, then create a health journal (see pages 24–25). With every over-the-counter medicine you take, every exercise class you join, and every muscle relaxant you try, you need to note how effective it was or wasn't. Most people find it easiest to organize the treatment part of their health journal by category: over-the-counter medications; prescription medications; lifestyle therapies; complementary therapies, such as massage and biofeedback. Just note down what you did or took, when, and how you felt afterward. In due time, this record will prove extremely helpful as you make your way toward a treatment plan that works for you.

Who's in Charge? You Are

If there's one goal Dr. Dennis Turk has when he works with people with fibromyalgia, it's this: He'd like them to stop thinking of themselves as patients. A clinical psychologist who heads the University of Washington School of Medicine's Fibromyalgia Research Center, Dr. Turk explains it this way:

"If you continue to think of yourself as a 'patient,' you'll depend upon a health care provider to get you better. What you have to start doing is to think of yourself as a person with a chronic syndrome. Since we don't have a cure, a great amount of what you have to do is take responsibility for yourself and learn about the things you can do to self-manage your syndrome." This subtle shift in thinking, he says, can make all the difference.

Dr. Turk is by no means alone in this view. Dr. Terence Starz uses nautical imagery to help his patients understand that he is not responsible for directing their health care; they are. A clinical professor of medicine at the University of Pittsburgh and practicing rheumatologist who treats many people with fibromyalgia, Dr. Starz tells his patients this: "You are the captain of the ship. You are in charge. Your doctor is the navigator whose job is to help chart a course and get you through stormy seas."

Over-the-counter relief
no cure, but a few hours of respite

Ask anyone with fibromyalgia about the most dominant symptom, and surely the first thing they will mention is the pain—the throbbing, acute, achy sensation felt in tender points and throughout their bodies. Some of the treatments for the pain are as close as your neighborhood pharmacy or supermarket.

What exactly are they? They are all classified as **analgesics**, drugs whose primary purpose is pain relief. Although not all pain is the same, the common factor is a sensory pathway from the affected area to the brain. Analgesics work at the level of the nerves, either by blocking the signal from the peripheral nervous system or by distorting the interpretation of the pain.

There are three main types of over-the-counter analgesics: aspirin, acetaminophen, and **NSAIDs**, or non-steroidal anti-inflammatory drugs.

◆ Aspirin relieves pain by inhibiting pain perception and by inhibiting the formation of pain-producing chemicals called **prostaglandins**. These prostaglandins are hormone-like substances present in body tissues that can cause inflammation and trigger the transmission of pain signals to the brain. Aspirin can affect the brain's heat-regulating center and thus can reduce fever.

◆ **Acetaminophen** is another over-the-counter pain reliever. No one knows exactly how acetaminophen works to relieve pain, but researchers believe that it works by blocking prostaglandins.

◆ **NSAIDs** inhibit the chemicals in the body that cause inflammation. Even though inflammation is not a symptom of fibromyalgia, some people with fibromyalgia find NSAIDs effective in managing the pain.

The Right Dosage Is Key

Many people mistakenly think that any pill or syrup sold over-the-counter is harmless. Not true! Dosage is key. That is why there are instructions on the back of every package that provide information about dosages. Don't ignore those instructions. Too much of any over-the-counter remedy can lead to serious health problems. This is especially true for those who are pregnant or who have kidney or liver disease.

◆ Aspirin should be limited to 3.4 grams or 8 tablets of 400 mg. a day. More than that amount can cause vertigo, tinnitus (ringing in the ears), nausea, vomiting, and coma.

◆ Acetaminophen should be limited to 4 grams or 8 tablets of 500 mg. a day. More than that amount can cause liver toxicity. Acetaminophen should not be used at all by those who consume three or more alcoholic drinks per day. That's because alcohol when mixed with acetaminophen is toxic to the liver.

◆ NSAIDs dosages are specific to each brand, since many different drugs are considered NSAIDs. Note: Overuse can lead to gastrointestinal bleeding, ulcers, and/or kidney damage. NSAIDs should not be used at all by those who consume three or more alcoholic drinks per day. That's because alcohol when mixed with NSAIDs is toxic to the liver.

Topical creams for pain
short-term relief

You can also try topical ointments for your muscle pain. For some with fibromyalgia, they offer immediate, temporary relief from muscular pain, generally with no side effects. For others, muscle ointments have little effect.

There are a number of over-the-counter gels, creams, liquids, spray-ons, and lotions that you apply directly where it hurts. Walk down the "pain relief" aisle of your local drug store, and you're likely to see a wide array of these products competing for your attention. Some of the more popular brands are Aspercreme, Ben Gay, Icy Hot, Deep Heating, Vicks VapoRub, Perform and Mineral Ice. Some contain a deep-heating ingredient called methyl salicylate, an aspirin-based substance. This drug may act in two ways: as a painkiller and also as an anesthetic when you massage it into your skin. Because this approach bypasses your stomach completely, you may find it more tolerable than swallowing a couple of aspirins, which can cause gastrointestinal upset in some people.

Other topical products contain capsaicin, the hot oil in chili peppers, which can temporarily modify joint or nerve pain. Capsaicin works by reducing your level of substance P (the neural hormone released by the neurons in the spinal cord to signal pain). It may take several applications before you feel any effect. Menthol, found in a few of these treatments, not only clears out your sinuses, but may also offer temporary relief from muscle pain. Peppermint oil, used mainly as a flavoring for candy, can also act as a topical painkiller.

Whether these products will offer you relief will depend upon the severity of your pain. If you do opt for a gel, wash it off before using a heat treatment. Otherwise, you risk burning yourself. It's a good idea to wash your hands after applying any of these muscle lotions or gels so you won't sting your eyes if you unconsciously rub them.

Pain medicine can make all the difference

I've never been a huge fan of medicine—any kind of medicine. In fact, I prided myself on taking nothing more than a multivitamin most of my adult life, while other women my age took handfuls of pills each day for this ailment or that. To tell you the truth, I was even a little smug about it! Well, that all changed after fibromyalgia was finally diagnosed a few years ago. When my doctor recommended muscle relaxants to help me to sleep better, I refused at first! I was convinced I could will it all away. Unfortunately, that didn't happen. So, only very reluctantly did I try the medicine, and I'm here to say that it's made a huge difference in my life and my outlook. I feel so much better and learned the hard way that there's nothing to be gained by being a martyr!

—Esther K., Glen Cove, NY

Injections for pain
short-term relief

A common treatment for trigger-point pain (from myofascial pain syndrome) are injections of a local anesthetic. These injections help the muscle to calm down. To that end, a number of doctors have been using injections to treat fibromyalgia. Here, tender points are injected with a local anesthetic, usually lidocaine. Initially, these injections can be quite painful and are used in only the most severe cases of persistent tender-point pain. The pain relief can last anywhere from several hours to several months, depending upon the individual. Note: There is no empirical published evidence that injections work for fibromyalgia.

Although their application in fibromyalgia is not well studied, injections of Botox are being used to treat fibromyalgia pain. When injected in small quantities, Botox causes selective weakening and paralysis of muscles, which alleviates spasms and pain. Doctors have used it to treat the muscular rigidity seen in various medical conditions, including cerebral palsy, strokes, multiple sclerosis, and myofascial pain syndrome. It was the successful use of Botox in people with severe myofascial pain syndrome that led doctors to try it for fibromyalgia. Some reports indicate that patients are getting relief that lasts anywhere from three to four months from injections of Botox into their tender points, but there is no empirical published evidence as yet. (Botox is best known now for its cosmetic use in loosening facial lines, temporarily giving a more youthful appearance.)

I'd like to try injections for my fibromyalgia. How do I go about getting them?

If you are seeking lidocaine injections, then your rheumatologist (see page 102) or physiatrist (see pages 104–105) can give them to you. But because Botox has yet to be given the green light for fibromyalgia, you will need to talk to your doctor about it. (Note: Just because Botox was approved by the FDA in the late 1980s for treatment for facial wrinkles, doesn't mean that it can be applied to all ailments.)

How often can I get injections?

It varies depending on the site and the substance being injected. Repetitive lidocaine injections are unlikely to be very harmful long-term, but tissue damage to the site can occur. Other chemicals, such as corticosteroids, can produce serious health problems if injected repeatedly. A general rule is no more than three injections per site per year to avoid tissue damage. Some physicians would restrict the number of injections, especially corticosteroids, to no more than three per site per lifetime.

If I have fibromyalgia, can I also have pain from trigger points?

Yes. Fibromyalgia often coexists with other pain disorders that can result in trigger-point pain. Trigger points are painful spots in the body that when touched radiate pain. Both trigger and tender points can be injected to help abate their pain.

Powerful prescriptions
but beware the side effects

You've tried the over-the-counter remedies and find they don't even dent your discomfort. What you need is something stronger, something available only through a prescription. While some people with fibromyalgia swear by prescription solutions, others claim the side effects are too severe to offset the pain relief. It can be a tricky balancing act. But with time and patience you should be able to find relief from most of your fibromyalgia pain.

A new class of these NSAIDs, or non-steroidal anti-inflammatory drugs, called **COX-2 specific inhibitors**, may offer more hope than the traditional over-the-counter variety, mainly because they are a bit less likely to cause stomach upset, gastrointestinal distress, or stomach ulcers than the over-the-counter COX-1 NSAIDs. Both COX-1 and COX-2 make prostaglandin, a substance that can stimulate inflammation.

Several anticonvulsants that are used to treat seizures in those who have epilepsy have been found to help with the pain of fibromyalgia in some people, though the mechanism of action is unclear. These include gabapentin (Neurontin), and topiramate (Topamax). Side effects of these drugs vary but may include nausea, rash, hair loss, fatigue, weight gain, weight loss, and liver problems.

Fibromyalgia Pain Medication

Type of Drug	Generic Name	Brand Name	Potential Side Effects
Cox-2 Inhibitors (also known as "Coxibs")	Celecoxib Rofecoxib	Celebrex Vioxx	Lightheadedness, nausea, heartburn, fluid retention, and kidney damage. If you have more than three alcoholic drinks per day, check with your doctor before taking any of these medications.
Anticonvulsants	Divalproex Sodium Valproic acid Gabapentin Topiramate	Depakote, Depakote ER Depakene Neurontin Topmax	Weight gain/loss, nausea, rash, liver problems

Opiates and narcotics
they can help when all else fails

Your pain has suddenly become unbearable. Your doctor suggests a narcotic, but you hesitate. You don't want to become a pain-pill addict, and you don't want to be drugged out, either. You are wrong on both accounts. Today's narcotics are designed to block severe pain and allow for all other life functions. The other good news is that when narcotic painkillers are used by those in severe pain, there is rarely an issue of dependency. When the pain abates, so does the need for the painkillers.

However, some doctors still do not recommend the use of narcotics for fibromyalgia patients. They fear the high risk of dependency despite evidence to the contrary. Others avoid prescribing narcotics because the side effects can be severe, from mental fuzziness to constipation, nausea, drowsiness, and even itching, which may be amplified in people with fibromyalgia. Other health care professionals argue that fibromyalgia patients should at least be given the chance to sample them for a trial period, especially during a **flare**—an acute episode of fibromyalgia pain.

Narcotic Fibromyalgia Medication

Generic Name	Brand Name	Potential Side Effects
Hydrocodone Bitartrate with acetaminophen	Vicodin Lortab Lorcet Hydrocet Dolacet	Rash, itchiness, constipation, tiredness or weakness, vomiting, feeling faint, nausea, dizziness, lightheadedness, drowsiness.
Oxycodone HCl	Oxycontin Roxicodone	Same as above
Propoxyphene hydrochloride	Darvon Wygesic	Nausea and vomiting, drowsiness, dizziness and lightheadedness

Treating depression
it often coexists with fibromyalgia

Fibromyalgia and depression often overlap. In fact, some researchers question whether it isn't depression that triggers fibromyalgia. Just why there is an association between these two conditions remains to be known.

What exactly is depression? The medical world describes it as a mixture of feelings of sadness for no apparent reason, loss of interest in life, and a sense of hopelessness. One key factor is how long these feelings persist. While we all may have moments of feeling blue, they usually go away in an hour or a day. Not so with a person who has a serious depression. Here the feelings persist, day after day, week after week, with very little respite.

There are degrees of depression. A mild depression is usually characterized by anxiety and varied moods—for example, a crying bout for no reason. A serious depression is marked by loss of appetite, difficulty sleeping, and an inability to concentrate.

The good news is that treatment for depression also helps with relieving fibromyalgia pain in some people. Tricyclic antidepressants, which have been traditionally prescribed for depression, also seem to help people with fibromyalgia cope more effectively with their pain. Some researchers theorize that tricyclic antidepressants change how pain is perceived. And because they can have a sedating effect, they help promote sleep, a common problem for people with fibromyalgia.

A newer category of antidepressants has shown promise at treating depression. These drugs are called **selective serotonin reuptake inhibitors** or SSRIs. In fibromyalgia patients, SSRIs also reduce fatigue, mental confusion, depression and pain, and they increase energy levels.

ASK THE EXPERTS

How do SSRIs work?

They prevent or inhibit the brain's breakdown (the reuptake) of serotonin, a "feel good" neurotransmitter (a primary chemical used in the brain). In doing so, the drug increases serotonin levels and therefore elevates your mood. The drug's ability to increase levels of serotonin is slow, so it takes about 14 days or more of regular use before its effect can be felt. SSRIs are not habit-forming and do not contain narcotics. Low doses usually work best for people with fibromyalgia.

Common Antidepressant Fibromyalgia Medication

Type of Drug	Generic Name	Brand Name	Potential Side Effects
Tricyclic antidepressants	Amitriptyline Doxepin Imipramine Nortriptyline	Elavil Sinequan Tofranil Pamelor	Sedation, weight gain, dry mouth, blurred vision, headache
SSRIs (selective serotonin re-uptake inhibitors)	Fluvoxamine Fluoxetine HCl Paroxetine HCl	Luvox Prozac Paxil	Sexual dysfunction, weight loss, nausea, sleepiness, and insomnia

Sleep medication
antidepressants can help

Because you hurt all over, you don't sleep well. When you don't sleep well, you awaken the next morning aching all over. You ache, so again tonight you don't sleep well. In order to feel better, you must break the cycle once and for all. Often, this can be accomplished by taking prescription tricyclic antidepressants (see pages 52–53), which relax your muscles and promote sleep. By inducing sleep, easing pain, and relaxing stiff muscles, tricyclics may help you to break out of the chronic pain and fatigue symptom cycle. Studies involving these drugs have shown mixed results, yet some people with fibromyalgia wouldn't dream of doing without them.

Better Sleeping Tips

If you sleep on your back, place a small, rolled towel inside the base of your pillowcase to avoid stressing your neck muscles. If you prefer to sleep on your stomach, don't turn your neck too far toward your shoulders or over-arch your back.

Sleep Medicine

Type of Drug	Generic Name	Brand Name
Sedatives	Temazepam	Restoril

Potential side effects for above:
Stomach upset, headache, depression, dizziness.

Type of Drug	Generic Name	Brand Name
Tricyclic Antidepressants	Amitriptyline HCl	Elavil
	Nortripyline HCl	Pamelor
	Doxepin	Sinequan

Potential side effects for above:
Difficulty concentrating, dizziness, drowsiness, dry mouth, headache, increased appetite, cravings for sweets, nausea, sleep disturbances, unpleasant taste, weight gain, urinary retention, weakness or tiredness.

Type of Drug	Generic Name	Brand Name
SRRIs	Paroxetine	Paxil
	Fluoxetine	Prozac
	Sertraline	Zoloft

Potential side effects for above:
Decrease in appetite or weight loss, decreased sexual drive or ability, diarrhea, drowsiness, worsening insomnia, dryness of the mouth.

Type of Drug	Generic Name	Brand Name
Muscle relaxants	Cyclobenzaprin	Flexeril

Potential side effects for above:
Dizziness or lightheadedness, drowsiness, dry mouth, confusion.

Exercise
why it really does work

Your muscles are aching and you are bone-tired. But your doctor is urging you to exercise, citing several conclusive studies that show exercise, especially aerobic exercise, helps relieve some of the symptoms of fibromyalgia. You protest and say that every time you have done anything remotely strenuous in the past, you suffered for days afterward with pain and exhaustion. Frankly, you are afraid to walk around the block. Exactly the point, says your doctor. The more you retreat from moving your body, the stiffer it becomes and the more fearful you become of injury and pain. It is a vicious circle that needs to be broken in order to help you get back on your feet again.

Few people realize that exercise has a specific role in the body. Its job is to deliver oxygen to the muscles, remove toxic metabolic waste that naturally builds up in the muscles, and repair soft tissue. Since most of this clean-up repair happens during sleep, a good night's rest is vital. Unfortunately, one of the main symptoms of fibromyalgia is fitful, unrestorative sleep. This may explain why people with fibromyalgia who start to exercise often report feeling worse the next day. Their fitful sleep did not give their body time to repair tissue damage from the previous day's exercise. The result is pain and muscle spasms upon waking.

You can break this circle of pain! According to Stacie Bigelow, author of *Fibromyalgia: Simple Relief Through Movement*, you need to first get your sleep problems squared away. A solid night's sleep is vital for everyone after exercising, but especially so for those with fibromyalgia. If you have been wary of trying sleep medication, you should reconsider. Just know that most sedatives are meant for short-term use only and are not appropriate for long-term use. Sedatives are best used as a bridge to allow for life-style changes and other interventions to work.

Getting started

Begin slowly and pace yourself. For those who have been inactive for a while, start with 10 minutes of gentle stretching a day. This type of stretching is slow and steady and *not* anything like the athletic stretches you might have seen runners do before a race or football players do before a game. (There are a number of stretching videos on the market that can help you get started. Two good ones are "AM and PM Stretch" and "Stretching with Bob Anderson." You can order these tapes through Collage Video, 800-433-6769.)

Once you have mastered the gentle art of stretching and it has become as second-nature as brushing your teeth in the morning, you can move on to aerobic exercise. This type of exercise is designed to get your heart muscles in shape. It usually calls for 15 to 20 minutes of sustained movement where your heart rate is slightly elevated. Start with swimming laps in a warm pool—a favorite exercise for those with fibromyalgia. If you don't live near a pool, consider other types of aerobic exercise, such as dancing, biking, rowing. You want to steer clear of the high-impact aerobic exercise class, as that type of exercise can be jarring to the joints.

Sure, it will take some self-discipline to get started, but once you do, exercise can become a delightful pleasure. In fact, studies show that aerobic exercise produces endorphins, the brain's natural painkillers, and they enhance the production of serotonin, boosting the brain's ability to control pain and moods. Why not tap into nature's own cure for your pain?

Cognitive-behavioral therapy
the glass can be half full

The relentlessness of chronic pain can easily wear down anyone's coping skills. But what a lot of people in pain don't realize is that how we think about pain can be just as powerful as the actual physical sensation of pain. That's where cognitive-behavioral therapy, or CBT, comes in. It is a form of short-term psychotherapy that emphasizes the vital role that thinking plays in how we interpret events and feelings to ourselves. This is especially true when it comes to dealing with pain. Take a look at these two statements: "My back is killing me again, I can't do anything, I am a failure" versus "My back is really hurting me, I will take it easy today and schedule a massage." The difference lies in interpretation of the pain and how you let it impact your life. In the first example, the person is engaging in what therapists would call "awfulizing," in which one event signals a global feeling of failure. In the second example, the same occurrence is viewed as simply that: one occurrence that needs to be addressed rationally. Some studies show that negative, globalizing thoughts about pain can be more destructive than the actual pain itself.

The solution is fairly simple—change how you think about the pain. Yes, it will take some effort, but it can be well worth it. CBT is based on the assumption that most emotional and behavioral reactions are learned. Therefore, its main goal is for you to un-learn your distorted mental reactions and replace them with more positive, realistic thoughts. For this reason, sessions in CBT are twofold. First, you and your therapist identify the "self-talk" in which you unwittingly engage throughout the day. For example: "If I don't clean this house up right now, my family will hate me." Once you start to see a pattern to your negative thinking and how it affects your mood and pain, the next step is to learn to see how distorted it is and replace it with something more realistic: "If I don't clean this house up right now, my family will understand. I will assign chores for the children to help with the cleaning."

ASK THE EXPERTS

How long does cognitive-behavioral therapy take?

Cognitive-behavioral therapy is considered among the quickest types of therapy in terms of the results clients obtain. The average number of sessions clients need is 16. Other forms of therapy, like psychoanalysis, can last for years. CBT therapists insist that it's effective because the therapy emphasizes instruction as well as homework assignments. CBT therapists believe that "just talking" is rarely enough to experience the relief you may be seeking. Rather, you need to learn a new set of thinking skills and more effective ways of behaving in your daily life.

Where can I find a therapist who knows cognitive-behavioral therapy?

You can contact the National Association of Cognitive-Behavioral Therapists. You can scan the group's Web site for a listing of names near you at **www.nacbt.org**.

You're entitled (to feel better)
yes, there is a pain-care bill of rights

Now that you understand why you feel pain, and are learning ways to more effectively explain it to your doctor, it's equally important to learn about your rights—that you are entitled to feel better!

"A lot of times, people with pain feel as though they have to bear it," says Yvette Colon, the director of education for the American Pain Foundation. "They feel they can't really ask the doctor questions about pain because the doctor will get mad at them, or they don't have the right to participate. That's wrong, and that's what our organization helps people to understand." (See resource box at chapter's end for contact information.) In fact, the organization has established a pain care "bill of rights," which can serve as a handy guide to what you can expect if you are in pain.

It is important to note that despite all pain treatments currently available, many people with fibromyalgia still continue to experience pain. That's why it is so important for people with fibromyalgia to take charge of their pain treatment. This is not an illness that your doctor can magically cure. It is a mysterious pain disorder that requires you to accept responsibility for getting better.

Pain-care bill of rights

As a person with pain, you have the right to:

◆ Have your report of pain taken seriously and be treated with dignity and respect by doctors, nurses, pharmacists, and other health care professionals.

◆ Have your pain thoroughly assessed and promptly treated.

◆ Be informed by your doctor about what may be causing your pain, about possible treatments, and the benefits, risks, and costs of each.

◆ Participate actively in decisions about how to manage your pain.

◆ Have your pain reassessed regularly and your treatment adjusted if your pain has not been eased.

◆ Be referred to a pain specialist if your pain persists (see page 106 for more about pain specialists).

◆ Get clear and prompt answers to your questions, take time to make decisions, and refuse a particular type of treatment if you choose.

Pain Factors

These things can make your pain feel worse:	*These things can block pain signals:*
◆ Stress	◆ Humor
◆ Overdoing physical activity	◆ Topical pain relievers
◆ Depression	◆ Distraction
◆ Anxiety	◆ Massage
◆ Fatigue	◆ Medication
◆ Focusing on pain	◆ Relaxation
	◆ Appropriate exercise
	◆ Heat and cold treatments

Helpful resources

The Chronic Pain Solution
by James N. Dillard, M.D.

Fibromyalgia: Simple Relief
Through Movement
by Stacie L. Bigelow, M.A.

The Arthritis Foundation
For more information on starting an
appropriate exercise program.
1330 West Peachtree Street
Atlanta, GA 30309
800-283-7800
www.arthritis.org

American Pain Foundation
111 South Salver St.
Baltimore, MD 21202
888-615-7246
www.painfoundation.org

American Chronic Pain
Association
P.O. Box 850
Rocklin, CA 95677
916-632-0922
www.theacpa.org

National Association of Cognitive
Behavioral Therapists
102 Gilson Avenue
P.O. Box 2195
Wierton, WV 26062
800-853-1135
www.nacbt.org

CHAPTER 4

Overlapping Syndromes

Chronic fatigue syndrome
striking similarities

Your fatigue is debilitating. Is it fibromyalgia or chronic fatigue syndrome? And can you have both at once? The answer is yes, you can have both, and that is often the case. Chronic fatigue syndrome, or CFS, is characterized by generalized fatigue (lasting longer than six months), sleep problems, concentration and short-term memory problems, sore throat, low-grade fevers, headaches, and tender lymph nodes. Like fibromyalgia, there is no known cause, though researchers think that either a flulike virus or an injury can trigger its onset. Often people who have CFS report that it began after they contracted a cold, bronchitis, hepatitis, mononucleosis, or an intestinal bug.

CFS affects both men and women of all ages and races. But women are two to four times as likely as men to get such a diagnosis. The best estimates are that half a million people in the United States have CFS. Because CFS symptoms are so similar to those of fibromyalgia, these two disorders are often confused.

As with fibromyalgia, there is no definitive diagnostic blood test to determine whether you have CFS. Instead, your doctor will ask you a series of questions to rule out other conditions. There is no cure yet for CFS, though there are various treatments available to mitigate its symptoms, starting with nonsteroidal anti-inflammatory drugs (NSAIDs), such as ibuprofen. For the longer term, the best that experts can suggest is that people who have CFS eat a nutritionally balanced diet, get lots of rest, exercise regularly, and try to avoid stress. Doctors sometimes prescribe antidepressants (see pages 52–53). In one four-city study by the Centers for Disease Control, about 50 percent of patients recovered, most of them within five years. Some people who have CFS recover completely, and some get progressively worse, while still others alternate between periods of illness and comparative well-being.

Symptoms of Chronic Fatigue Syndrome

Noticeable anxiety and excitability

Mood swings, including bouts of crying

Irritability and impatience

Impaired memory

Inability to concentrate

Loss of interest in normal activities

Confused thinking

Depression

Loss of interest in sex

Withdrawal from friends and family

Dysregulation Spectrum Syndrome

Because fibromyalgia shares a number of similar symptoms with other disorders, a researcher named Dr. Muhammad Yunus has a theory that there is one disorder behind them all. He calls it dysregulation spectrum syndrome and says it accounts for fibromyalgia, chronic fatigue syndrome, myofascial pain syndrome, as well as the suffering caused by multiple chemical sensitivity syndrome. He thinks the problem behind these overlapping disorders lies in the dysregulation of the neurohormonal system—in other words, faulty body chemistry.

Myofascial pain syndrome
muscles as tight as a drum

Myofascial pain syndrome is a pain disorder that affects the muscles and the fascia or connective tissue that surrounds and supports them. Myofascial pain syndrome usually occurs after an injury or prolonged pain, say from arthritis, though it can be set off by something as simple as poor posture, or muscle strain caused by unequal leg lengths, or too-quick movement from an awkward or static position. Other potential causes include psychological stress and chronic infection. Predisposing conditions include deficiencies of calcium, potassium, iron, and some vitamins, as well as underactive thyroid, elevated uric acid, and low blood sugar.

Whatever the reason, injury or pain causes the muscles to tighten, which in turn causes a buildup of lactic acid and other metabolic wastes. In due time, nerves become irritated so that muscles tighten even more, which can create painful **trigger points** (a knot or taut band of muscle) that when pressed radiate pain to other parts of the body. (Trigger points differ from tender points; see pages 16–17.) A diagnosis of myofascial pain syndrome is determined if you feel pain when pressure is applied to various trigger points. The pain can come in different forms, such as aching, stabbing, burning, and nagging.

Myofascial pain syndrome occurs in men and women of all ages, more often among those who live sedentary lives than those who exercise regularly. And as with other chronic pain conditions, myofascial pain is sometimes accompanied by lasting fatigue and depression. Myofascial pain syndrome can be eased by releasing the muscle through stretches, massage, and exercise, or sometimes by directly addressing the cause, for instance with heel lifts or ergonomically correct workstations. Sometimes a doctor will inject a local anesthetic directly into the primary trigger points, which usually also brings relief to satellite trigger points in the same region. Steroids can help in areas of inflammation. Muscle relaxants and NSAIDs (nonsteroidal anti-inflammatory drugs) may ease the pain when combined with an active exercise program. The earlier treatment is begun, the better the prognosis. In difficult cases, doctors sometimes use a combination of physical therapy, trigger-point injections, and massage.

Ask the Experts

Why does the doctor apply pressure in one place when the pain is in another place?

That's the funny thing about trigger points. The pain you feel may be in an entirely different place than its source. This is known as **referred pain.** There are even four different kinds of trigger points: active trigger points, tender spots in the same general area as the source of the pain; latent trigger points, dormant areas that can flare up anytime; secondary trigger points, as a spot in one muscle that becomes active because of overload in another; and satellite trigger points, which are located in the same area as other trigger points.

I experience acute muscle pain in my jaws whenever I chew. Is that myofascial pain syndrome?

No. That is a symptom of **temporomandibular joint disorder.** It is a disorder that results in pain upon opening the mouth. People who have it report feeling as if their jaw is out of alignment—though it is not. The cause is unknown, though stress plays a key role. It used to be treated with jaw surgery, but that proved ineffective. Doctors now treat it with analgesics, and sometimes injections of lidocaine or cortisone into the jaw joint. Some prescribe mouth guards, which can help you keep from grinding your teeth at night and thus lessen the tension in your jaw.

Polymyalgia
another pain syndrome

Polymyalgia rheumatica (PMR) can sneak up on you as unthreateningly as an overnight pain in the neck. It is characterized by moderate-to-severe morning pain and stiffness not only in the neck, but also in the shoulders, upper arms, hips, thighs, and knees (at least two of those areas). It can develop suddenly or gradually and be accompanied by fatigue, weight loss, and a slight fever. Like polymyalgia, doctors do not know what causes it. They have determined, however, that it is almost exclusively a disease of aging, attacking one person out of 200 over age 50 and at an average age of 70. Women are twice as likely to get it as men, and although people of any race can be affected, most of those afflicted are white, especially those of Northern European or Scandinavian ancestry.

Mild cases may be treated with nonsteroidal anti-inflammatory drugs (NSAIDs) such as ibuprofen; more painful ones with low doses of the powerful anti-inflammatory corticosteroid prednisone. If not treated, PMR usually disappears in one to four years. Stretching and low-impact exercises—such as swimming, walking, and bicycling—often help.

More seriously, 15 to 25 percent of people who have PMR also have **giant cell arteritis** (also known as **temporal arteritis**), an inflammation of walls of the arteries, primarily in the temples, but also in the neck and arms. The inflammation and swelling can cause the arteries to narrow, reducing blood flow. Symptoms include severe headaches, jaw pain, and vision problems, as well as a tender, swollen temporal artery with a reduced pulse. A biopsy will show abnormal cells in the artery walls. Giant cell arteritis can lead to permanent blindness or stroke or both. It is important that it be diagnosed and treated early, usually with high-dose corticosteroids. Giant cell arteritis can develop simultaneously with PMR or after it disappears.

What tests can the doctor order for polymyalgia?

The most common test is for the so-called "sed" rate, for elevated erythrocyte sedimentation. The test measures how long it takes red blood cells to sink to the bottom of a test tube. If they do so quickly, that is an indication of inflammation in the body. However, because inflammation is also a symptom of many forms of rheumatic and other diseases, the doctor will need additional tests to rule out those other conditions.

I heard of a disease called Sjogren-Larsson syndrome. Is that like fibromyalgia?

Not really. **Sjogren syndrome** is a disorder of the connective tissue, much like rheumatoid arthritis, scleroderma, and polymyositis. Its main symptoms are dry skin, eyes, nose, and mouth. It results in difficulty chewing and swallowing. Treatment calls for moisturizing the skin and nose and using artificial drops for the eyes.

For a while there my doctor thought I had Raynaud's phenomenon. What is that?

Raynaud's phenomenon is the periodic interruption of blood flow to the fingers, toes, ears, and nose. This can cause painful tingling and burning sensations. The attacks are often associated with other disorders such as rheumatoid arthritis and lupus. If Raynaud's phenomenon symptoms continue for at least two years and there is no other disorder or disease involved, then it is called **Raynaud's disease**. Treatment involves blood-vessel-widening drugs and protecting the body from cold. Biofeedback (see pages 142–143) has also been shown to be effective.

Irritable bowel syndrome
How to handle those gastric upsets

Irritable bowel syndrome, or IBS, is a common disorder of the intestines that leads to crampy pain, gassiness, bloating and changes in bowel habits. People with fibromyalgia also have symptoms of IBS. Some people experience constipation, others have diarrhea, and still others experience both. Over the years, IBS has been known by many names—colitis, mucous colitis, spastic colon, spastic bowel, and functional bowel disease.

The exact cause of IBS is not known, nor is there a cure for it. Like fibromyalgia, doctors call it a **functional disorder** because there is no sign of disease when the colon is examined. While IBS may cause a great deal of discomfort and distress, it does not cause permanent harm to the intestines and does not lead to intestinal bleeding or to a serious disease such as cancer. Often it is just a mild annoyance, but for some people with more extreme cases, it can be disabling. They may not be able to go out to work, attend social functions, or even travel short distances.

Some experts speculate that IBS, like fibromyalgia, involves a flaw in the body's nervous system and its response to stress. Although they are not exactly certain why this flaw happens, they do acknowledge that emotions influence our bodies. Specifically, stress affects our hormones, which in turn impact our bodies and the way they function.

Many IBS sufferers say their symptoms worsen when they are under stress. Not surprisingly, stress stimulates colonic spasms in people with IBS. While this process is not entirely understood, scientists point out that the colon is partially controlled by the nervous system. Simply understanding that IBS is not a serious or life-threatening condition may relieve anxiety and stress.

What can I do to help with my IBS?

Large meals can cause cramping and diarrhea. Your symptoms may be eased if you eat smaller meals more often or just eat less at regular meals. You might also try to increase your dietary fiber intake, which can lessen IBS symptoms in many cases. Whole-grain breads and cereals, beans, fruits, and vegetables are excellent sources of fiber. High-fiber diets keep the colon mildly distended, which may help to prevent spasms from developing. Some forms of fiber also keep water in the stools, thereby preventing hard stools that are difficult to pass. It is also vital to drink plenty of fluids, at least 10 glasses of water a day. Regular aerobic exercise is also helpful.

Are there any medications that treat IBS?

Not yet. There are only medicines to treat various symptoms of IBS. For example, if muscle spasms are your chief complaint, your doctor may prescribe either hyoscyamine sulfate (brand names are Anaspaz, Cystopaz, Levsin) or dicyclomine (brand names are Bentyl, Di-Spaz) to relax spasms in the colon. Heating pads and warm baths can also offer comfort. When diarrhea is a frequent problem, medicine such as loperamide (brand name Imodium) may be helpful. Your doctor may recommend fiber supplements or laxatives if you are constipated.

Getting Help

Some experts recommend keeping a food journal and noting which foods seem to aggravate the symptoms. In addition, you may want to seek out a registered dietician (see pages 128–129) or a nutritionist to help you make wise food choices and design your meals accordingly.

Helpful resources

The Merck Manual of Medical Information
Mark H. Beers, M.D.
Editor-in-Chief

From Fatigued to Fantastic!: A Proven Program to Regain Vibrant Health Based on a New Scientific Study Showing Highly Effective Treatment for Chronic Fatigue and Fibromyalgia
by Jacob Teitelbaum, M.D.

International Foundation for Functional Gastrointestinal Disorders
P.O. Box 170864
Milwaukee, WI 53217
414-964-1799
www.iffgd.org

The Arthritis Foundation
1330 West Peachtree Street
Atlanta, GA 30309
800-283-7800
www.arthritis.org

Children with Fibromyalgia

Fibromyalgia in children
more than just growing pains

Just as with adults, children and teenagers can get fibromyalgia. It is predominantly teenagers who get it rather than young children. It usually affects girls between the ages of 13 and 15. There is no known cause, though doctors suspect it can follow on the heels of an illness or an injury.

The symptoms are similar to adult fibromyalgia: diffuse pain, morning stiffness, headaches, and fatigue. And just like adults, affected children are extra-sensitive at certain tender-point areas in the soft tissue of the neck, back, chest, and buttocks. These tender points are specific spots in the body where the muscle connects with bone. There are 18 tender points in the body that seem to be exquisitely sensitive to those with fibromyalgia. To make a diagnosis of fibromyalgia, a doctor applies about nine pounds of pressure (what it would take to push a stuck doorbell) on each point. In adults, if 11 out of those 18 points result in pain, then a diagnosis of fibromyalgia is given. In children, however, only 8 to 10 painful tender points are necessary for a diagnosis of **juvenile fibromyalgia**. Because the American College of Rheumatology has developed criteria for diagnosing the syndrome in adults only, doctors aren't certain if these criteria are also valid for children. Nevertheless, Dr. Muhammad B. Yunus of the University of Illinois College of Medicine, identified the following symptoms:

- ◆ chronic headaches
- ◆ morning fatigue
- ◆ stiffness
- ◆ irritable bowel syndrome
- ◆ generalized aches and pains

Dr. Yunus also noted that poor sleep, significant family dysfunction, and depression are common among children with the syndrome.

Is fibromyalgia hereditary?

There may be a hereditary component. In one small study, 28 percent of children whose mothers had fibromyalgia also developed the disorder. Another study noted that 66 percent of parents of children with fibromyalgia reported some kind of chronic pain, and about 10 percent had fibromyalgia itself. But these studies are too small to draw significant conclusions. What is interesting is that some adults with fibromyalgia recall being unusually fatigued as preteens or teenagers and are fairly certain that the cause was fibromyalgia.

Children and Fibromyalgia

It's called juvenile fibromyalgia, and while it's rare, some studies have shown that it's increasing.

♦ In one study, 1.2 percent of schoolchildren, all girls, met the criteria for fibromyalgia.

♦ Another study reported that fibromyalgia typically develops in children after age 13, and was most commonly diagnosed at age 15.

♦ The Arthritis Foundation reports that fibromyalgia is becoming increasingly prevalent in adolescents, more evidence of a possible connection between the disorder and hormones.

♦ While symptoms of fibromyalgia are similar in young people to those of adult sufferers, from the aches to the fatigue, the outcome appears better for children than for adults. Many children outgrow the disorder or report fewer or less acute symptoms as they get older.

Treatments for teens
different solutions

The good news is that your child is not suffering from a degenerative illness, but the bad news is that the pain, stiffness, depression, and fatigue are signs of a chronic disorder for which a cure has yet to be found. The only thing doctors can do is treat the symptoms. The treatments for fibromyalgia in teenagers are similar to what an adult would get and are just as varied, and as with adults, depression can coexist with fibromyalgia. It is important to address and treat the depression as well as the fibromyalgia.

Depending on your doctor, your child may be prescribed low doses of over-the-counter medicines such as NSAIDs for pain and perhaps an antihistamine like Benadryl to help with sleep. If your child's symptoms are severe, your doctor may suggest more powerful prescription medicines for the pain and sleep problems. There are also other treatment options that call for a combination of physical therapy, oral or injected glucocorticoids (see page 46) and cognitive-behavioral therapy (see pages 58–59). If depression is a factor, then low doses of antidepressants may be prescribed.

Because sports and outdoor activities can play such an important role in a child's life, it is important to factor that into your child's treatment. The pain of fibromyalgia can make some children afraid to run or jump or try out for a favorite sport. Explain to your child that he or she needs to do gentle stretches before starting an activity to "warm up the muscles". Exercise is such a key component to treatment (see pages 56–57) that it should be encouraged at all times.

When it comes to organized sports, however, it's best to consult your doctor about what is appropriate for your child. Much will depend upon your child's fitness levels and how well he or she can cope with the pressure of competing. It is important to tell your child that a fibromyalgia flare-up can sideline a person for a day or two and that is okay.

ASK THE EXPERTS

How do I talk to my child about her illness?

Start with the good news: She is going to be fine. Explain that her muscle pain and fatigue are due to a pain disorder called fibromyalgia that is not going to affect her health. Better still, her symptoms will get better with treatment. A word of caution: Children are especially vulnerable to thinking that anything that goes wrong is their fault. It's critical to stress that fibromyalgia is no one's fault, that nothing anyone said or did or did not do could have prevented it. Explain that there are medicines and special therapies that will help her to feel better. While no medicine exists that will make it go away (and this is important to stress), she can do many things to make herself feel well and strong. Mention too that she will have good and bad days, and will need to tell those around her what she needs when she's not feeling so great.

Keeping a Log

It will take time before you hit upon the right treatment for your child's fibromyalgia. Most doctors will suggest that you keep a log of your child's symptoms and how she responds to the various treatments. You can be the keeper of the log, or your child can do it. You both have several choices: You can keep it simple and create a chart and post it on the fridge so you or your child can update it daily after each medicine. If your child is a teenager, you might also want to get a journal or diary she can keep to record her feelings, a fibro diary of sorts. This can be a spiral notebook or an elaborate hard-bound journal in which she records her thoughts and feelings, such as anger and frustration, about her illness. (Some studies show that writing down your feelings about your illness helps boost the immune system).

How families react
a chronic illness can affect everyone

The worry never seems to end. How, you wonder, will your child's fibromyalgia influence the way she grows up? Will she be able to keep up with her peers, participate in ordinary childhood activities? Will she be stigmatized and misunderstood, shunned by other children because she "acts sick, but doesn't look it"?

And what about your other children? It's not uncommon for a younger brother or sister to resent the amount of time and energy devoted to a sick child. Some siblings will even feign illness in a ploy for attention. Others act out or withdraw, becoming eerily quiet and sometimes surly.

You'd also be less than honest if you or your spouse denied that sometimes you resent the whole thing. You're tired of constantly reminding your child to take her medicine. You're frustrated by the number of times you've had to bow out of events, cancel vacation, and postpone visits from family members all because your child is suffering a flare-up and can't endure any added stimulation. If you do feel overwrought, stressed, or even despairing at times, you are only normal. A chronic illness is a huge stressor on a family. Yet it is important to keep stress to a minimum. Learn to talk about your feelings and share your concerns. During especially stressful times, consider having the whole family meet with a family therapist, who can help each member talk about particular worries and concerns.

I am so worried about my child getting hurt during sports that I can't bear to have him play. When should I let him play?

"One of the biggest mistakes parents make," says Dr. Patrick McGrath, a professor of psychology, pediatrics, and psychiatry at Dalhousie University in Halifax, Nova Scotia, "is feeling sorry for their child and sheltering them from everyday living, exempting the ill child from chores, or keeping him home from events and activities." While this reaction is normal, "there's no merit in feeling sorry for a child with fibromyalgia," he warns. "It only robs them of their dignity. They're not to be pitied. They're to be admired for their courage. Your major goal is for your child to have as normal a life as possible in spite of the pain."

FIRST PERSON INSIGHTS

I am not a hypochondriac!

The first thing I do when I wake up, before I go to high school? Take a nice, hot bath! I am so achy and stiff each morning, I have to coax myself to get up and out of bed. The bath and some gentle stretches which my physical therapist taught me help a lot.

But at least now my mom and I know what we're dealing with. When the doctors finally ruled out juvenile rheumatoid arthritis and gave me a diagnosis of fibromyalgia, I was so scared! I had never heard of the disease before. My grandmother is still convinced I am a hypochondriac because I have so many things wrong with me. But I am learning more and more about how to deal with this strange illness of mine. Now I can pace myself and do all the right things to keep the symptoms away.

It's also hard for me to figure out who to tell. Most of my friends know about my fibromyalgia, and they're cool with it. They 'get it' when I'm too exhausted to go out after a football game. One friend is really great about encouraging me to rest up before we all go out on a weekend. I don't know what I'd do without my friends!

—Brittany S., Plano, TX

Practical matters
tips for parents, teens, and others

Parents: Before the school year begins, schedule an appointment with the school's guidance counselor, the principal, and the school nurse or health office. You'll want to make them all fully aware of your child's syndrome. Don't be surprised if you are met with blank stares or perhaps even skepticism. Misunderstanding and ignorance about fibromyalgia are still rampant, especially when it comes to children.

You'll want to give the school authorities a rundown of the symptoms your child experiences and how they affect him ("He's usually groggy in the mornings, more alert as the day wears on . . .")

Teenagers: Be prepared. Arm yourself with information about fibromyalgia. Have a list of key Web addresses or helpful sites handy that you can share with your teachers and counselors.

Teens and preteens who have fibromyalgia say it's important to stay active outside of school, whether in low-key sports or special-interest groups or clubs. If you work for extra cash, try to find a job that's not physically demanding, for instance selling tickets at a movie theatre rather than mowing lawns.

If your peers tease you, try to remain neutral or use humor as a weapon. Finding friends who understand and bolster you is very important, too, whether they come from an organized support group or are just naturally sympathetic and understanding friends.

Sometimes, small things can make a big difference at school. Things like:

◆ Have an extra set of books at home, so you don't have to lug heavy stuff back and forth.

◆ If you can get an extra locker at school, you won't have to carry all your books at one time, and you can deposit them between classes. Or ask a friend if you can use his or her locker space.

◆ A laptop computer makes it easier to take in-class notes. When you are especially tired, ask the teacher or a sympathetic classmate for notes or a summary of the material covered.

◆ Make your teachers aware of your situation, so that if you have difficulty arriving on time, they understand the reason. Similarly, knowing about your fibromyalgia will help them to understand why you are fidgety or sluggish in class.

◆ If you can, schedule your classes in such a way that you don't have to walk too far between classrooms or buildings.

◆ Schedule a study hall first thing in the morning, if that's your hardest time of day. Or if you tire more easily by the day's end, schedule it for then.

Helpful resources

Raising a Child with Arthritis
by The Arthritis Foundation.
800-283-7800
www.arthritis.org

Juvenile Arthritis Foundation
This is a council of the Arthritis
Foundation devoted to serving the
special needs of children, teens, and
young people with childhood rheumatic diseases. (Be sure to check out
the message boards for parenting
topics, as well as the areas targeted
specifically for children.)
404-965-7538
www.arthritis.org

**The National Fibromyalgia
Association**
2200 N. Glassell Street, Suite A
Orange, CA 92865
714-921-0150
www.fmaware.org

**Friends International Support
for Fibromyalgia, Chronic Pain
and more.**
This is an excellent place
to hook up with and learn from
others who may be experiencing
what you are. Type "fibromyalgia"
in their search box.
www.ezboard.com

The Pediatric Network
www.pediatricnetwork.org

To learn more about the Individuals
with Disabilities in Education Act or
to find valuable links, visit:
www.ideapractices.org

CHAPTER 6

Using the Internet

Evaluating Web sites
telling what's good from what's not

You have been given a diagnosis and perhaps even begun your treatment. If you are like most people, your first instinct is to find out everything there is to know about fibromyalgia. This is a useful instinct, so hold on to it. You don't need to become an expert on fibromyalgia—your goal is to become informed and active. After seeing their doctor, most people go home and turn on their computer and start in. You can too. But first a word of advice: Not all information on the Web is accurate. The sites you find may contain outdated facts, misinformation, poor research, urban legends, propaganda, and outright lies. How can you tell what's good and what is not? Use this checklist:

1. Check the date. In a book or newspaper, you can always see the publication date—so you know whether the information is current. On the Web, not every page carries the publication date. The better medical sites do. If you don't see a date, don't trust any figures the page calls "current."

2. Check the source. Most articles online have bylines giving the writer's name. If you have not heard of the writer, feed the name into a search engine and see who else carries the byline. A good medical paper always backs up its statements with sources and bibliographies. Check any article for sources and links to other sites.

3. Check the publisher. Look at the Web address of any article you are evaluating. Is it a name you recognize—a well-known clinic or foundation or government site? If not, look around for a link labeled "About this site" or something like that, and see who is behind it all.

4. Don't be put off by advertising. Advertising is a fact of life on the Web. One exception: If a site seems to be selling something in its articles, move on. You cannot trust advertorials on television, so don't trust your health to them online.

Searching Smart

Bookmark important pages.
Great, you have just hit a page with handy links and lots of good solid information. Instead of stopping to write down the name of the site, save time and bookmark it! Every Web browser lets you save the names of favorite Web pages. All you have to do is be on the Web page you want to note, go up to the toolbar, and click on the correct tab that will tell your computer to make a snapshot of the site. In Internet Explorer, click on Favorites; in America Online, click on Favorite Places; and in Netscape, click on Bookmarks. Next time you want to access that page, all you need to do is look through your list of favorite sites or bookmarks and click on it.

Print and file essential information.
When you find a page with a lot of relevant information on it, print it out and file it in your health journal (see page 24). As the number of printouts grows, you can categorize them by topic: medicine, specialists, alternative therapies, and so on. This will make it easier to find the information. Remember, too, that you don't have to print a whole Web page. Highlight just the bit that interests you, click on File, then Print, and in the Print box, click on Selection. Then click on the OK button or "Apply" and you'll have a nice short printout.

Make every search count
It's important to use precise search terms, or keywords. The more words you type in, the more specific your search will be. Entering more keywords increases the relevance of what you get in return, but also limits the number of returns you'll see. Try a broad search first, then narrow down the results by adding search terms.

Each search engine typically has a link that takes you to an "advanced" search form. There you can refine your search by entering words you do not want to see—for instance, excluding the word "depression" if you want to read about only the physical aspects of fibromyalgia.

Put quotes around words that should appear next to each other, and the search engine will treat them as one word. Searching for "disability insurance" will help you find pages that refer to that specific type of insurance, rather than pages that cover insurance in general.

Top layman fibromyalgia sites
How not to be overwhelmed

You are armed and ready to go. But first, one more piece of advice—don't start by searching the main search engines such as AltaVista (**www.alta vista.com**) or Google (**www.google.com**) for information about fibromyalgia. Why? Because you can be overwhelmed with the number of sites you'll see listed and not know where to start. Instead, start with the fibromyalgia-specific sites listed below to ground you in the basics about fibromyalgia. If you don't have Internet access at home, try your public library—many libraries have Internet access stations that you can use for half an hour or more at a time. The following sites provide comprehensive fibromyalgia information and are frequently updated:

www.fmnetnews.com
With daily updates, this Fibromyalgia Network site contains easy-to-understand explanations for fibromyalgia symptoms, methods used to treat them, links to many other sites, physician referrals, and more. The organization publishes a newsletter you can order online.

www.immunesupport.com
The granddaddy of them all, this busy site boasts three million visitors annually and, not surprisingly, bills itself as "the world's largest fibromyalgia Web site." It offers access to more than 3,000 fibromyalgia and chronic fatigue syndrome articles and abstracts, a tip of the day, extensive message boards, a "fibro chat" area; a "coping corner," links to many other sites, and more (including lots of ads).

www.myalgia.com
Sponsored by the Oregon Fibromyalgia Foundation, this site is worth a visit for its sections on herbal and dietary solutions for symptoms, referrals to relevant literature, and up-to-date research. It even offers a fascinating section on Mexican artist Frida Kahlo, who is said to have had fibromyalgia.

www.fibromyalgia.com

Billed as "an online pain management resource," the site has a section on Frequently Asked Questions, chat areas, and clear definitions. It even has a section on the "fibro five": irritable bowel syndrome, chronic fatigue syndrome, fibromyalgia, migraine headache, and interstitial cystitis.

www.paincare.org

The nonprofit National Foundation for the Treatment of Pain is dedicated to providing support for patients suffering from "intractable" pain, as well as for their families, friends, and physicians. The organization's Web site offers much information on the legal aspects of pain treatment and patients' rights.

www.partnersagainstpain.com

With special sections for patients and their caregivers, medical professionals, and institutions, this site offers medical definitions, information on drugs and other treatments, as well as articles on pain management and a helpful pain assessment test. You can also find links here to pain-support communities as well as a suggested reading list.

Top medical sites
go to these for clinical information

Once you have a basic grounding in your fibromyalgia, you'll be ready to sink your teeth into more detailed information. Again, avoid doing a general search; go instead to the established medical sites. There are two basic types: those maintained by a specific medical school or clinic, and the big medical search engines that are supported by the U.S. government.

MedLine and the National Institutes of Health

www.nlm.nih.gov/medline/plus/fibromyalgia.html

Excellent, reliable general information on fibromyalgia, with easy-to-understand definitions, coping tips, links to other relevant sites, updates on clinical trials, and an interactive tutorial. Some sections are available in Spanish. This site is sponsored by the National Library of Medicine and the National Institutes of Health

American Academy of Family Physicians

www.aafp.org or the slightly more user-friendly **www.familydoctor.org**
 Both sites are sponsored by the same organization. Both offer solid information for patients (with sections for professionals, including residents and students) with reader-friendly definitions, and articles that span everything from the best exercise plan to an overview of treatment options.

Journal of the American Medical Association (JAMA)

www.jama.ama-assn.org

The Web site for this esteemed publication is updated daily and contains excellent abstracts on various aspects of fibromyalgia.

Mayo Clinic

www.mayoclinic.com

The subtitle says it all: "Reliable information for a healthier life." This easy-to-navigate site from a well-respected institution offers comprehensive information not only on fibromyalgia and related syndromes and afflictions, but also on virtually any health issue, from living with chronic pain to finding the right doctor, as well as explanations on complementary and alternative medicines.

The Arthritis Foundation
www.arthritis.org
An attractive, easy-to-navigate, easy-to-comprehend site brimming with practical information, tips, and resources on arthritis and its offshoots, such as fibromyalgia.

The American College of Rheumatology
www.rheumatology.org
With sections geared for both patients and medical professionals, this site offers solid explanations and definitions on fibromyalgia, as well as a national directory of rheumatologists.

Harvard Health Publications
www.health.Harvard.edu
Updated daily, this site offers some helpful fibromyalgia abstracts gleaned from research.

Physician's Desk Reference (PDR)
www.healthsquare.com
Geared mainly toward women, this exceptionally reader-friendly site contains explanations for just about any condition, disease, or syndrome you can name, including fibromyalgia.

Researching doctors
where to find the right medical help

Because fibromyalgia is a comparatively new—or newly identified—syndrome, finding the right doctor is even more important for people who have it than for those with other ailments. Many health professionals are still not fully aware of the scope of this disorder. These physicians may insist your symptoms are "stress-related" or all in your head, then scribble a prescription for antidepressants and send you on your way.

The place to begin your quest is the grapevine. Ask people in your support group or fibromyalgia circles for recommendations. If you're not part of a group, and even if you are, you can still benefit from an Internet search. A Net search can't reveal a doctor's bedside manner or level of compassion, but it can turn up his or her educational background and professional credentials, such as board certification, as well as any disciplinary actions taken against the doctor.

Before you begin, it's a good idea to call your health insurer to find out which health care providers are in your plan. Most people now have a limited number of providers they can see. If you don't find any suitable doctors in your plan, find out the plan's policy for going "out of network."

The American College of Rheumatology

www.rheumatology.org

Most experts agree that rheumatologists are among the best-trained specialists to deal with fibromyalgia. On this site, you can find a rheumatologist in the U.S. by individual state or overseas.

The American Medical Association (AMA)

www.ama-assn.org

You can search for information, including educational background, on a physician based upon medical specialty, name, or location.

American Board of Medical Specialties (ABMS)

www.abms.org

This is an organization of 24 medical specialty boards that will tell you whether a doctor is board-certified or board-eligible in a particular area. "Board-certified" means a doctor has completed two additional years of training and has passed a national examination. "Board-eligible" means that the training, but not the test, has been completed.

Pain Net, Inc.

www.painnet.com

Describing itself as "the J.D. Power, Nielsen Ratings, Consumer Reports of Pain," this organization advocates a more comprehensive approach to pain management. It also offers a state-by-state listing of doctors, dentists, therapists chiropractors, pharmacists, and counselors with training and education in treating painful diseases and conditions.

The Beehive

www.thebeehive.org

Enter your location, choose the type of doctor you need, and plug in your insurance provider, and you will get a list of appropriate physicians and information on how to contact them.

National Mental Health Association

www.nmha.org

This is the country's oldest and largest nonprofit organization addressing all aspects of mental health, with more than 340 affiliates nationwide. Its resource center provides referrals for local treatment centers and lists of mental health providers. It includes a toll-free hotline (800-969-6642).

Online support
welcome to a world where everyone has fibromyalgia

It's natural that the only people who can fully understand all that you're going through are others who have the same disorder. At any time of the day or night, you can instantly hook up with a community of people who also have fibromyalgia or care for those who do. Many sites offer chat rooms, or message boards, where you can sound off if you feel like it or just listen in if you prefer. You can e-mail or post a message about some aspect or another of fibromyalgia, and you will likely get a barrage of responses. If you want to ask about the merits of a new drug or treatment your doctor has recommended, just beware that there is no quality control on the Internet. Anyone can advocate for products for fibromyalgia without any scientific evidence. Online support is best for more practical tips, such as how to get a good night's rest or how others who have fibromyalgia cope with the demands of young children. If you have concerns such as these, then you've come to the right place.

First, though, spend a few minutes browsing through sites with boards and communities. Wander through the topics that are dominating the boards. If the subjects grab you, then carefully follow the specific site's directions for how to participate.

Some may require that you sign in or log on before you can take part. This may mean you need to create a new sign-on name, which may be something other than your e-mail address.

Remember to follow the rules set forth by that community. Some ask that you stick to the medical aspects of fibromyalgia only, while others invite dialogue on just about anything.

Note: It's not prudent to reveal much about yourself (address, phone number, real name) to someone you've just met online, even on a well-established fibromyalgia site. So take your time—go slow.

Fibrohugs

www.fibrohugs.com

A warm, cozy, layman site that offers some clinical explanations and medical updates but primarily supports fibromyalgia patients and their loved ones. It offers extensive, very active chat areas. It's run by people with fibromyalgia and bills itself as one of the most visited fibromyalgia sites. "We know exactly what you need: you need fibro 'hugs'."

HealingWell

www.healingwell.com

This site ("on diseases, disorders, and chronic illness") is updated daily and offers community resources, and information galore, including articles on everything from the healing art of massage to interacting with your doctor. It is especially focused on the emotional side of chronic illness.

UKFibromyalgia

www.Ukfibromyalgia.com

This site has excellent discussion forums, as well as great explanations about the syndrome and related conditions, all with a British twist.

Immunesupport

www.immunesupport.com

Billing itself as "the world's largest fibromyalgia Web site," this site offers multitudinous opportunities to post messages, hook up with others, and gain a sense of community.

iVillage

www.ivillage.com

Calling itself "the women's network—busy women sharing solutions and advice," this site has outstanding message boards and chat areas specifically geared for those with fibromyalgia. It also contains easy-to-digest medical information, personal stories, and links to newsletters and articles.

Newsgroups
freewheeling give-and-take

Newsgroups are essentially collections of e-mails, stored online for you to browse. They are often more freewheeling than the discussion forums on Web sites. You can "post" your own message by e-mailing it to the newsgroup. An easy way to access newsgroups is to click on Google's "Groups" tab, then enter "fibromyalgia." (On the opposite page, you'll see how to view newsgroups, step-by-step.) Newsgroups are also a place to learn from mistakes, pick up advice, and post your own so that others can benefit.

As you start to scan the groups, you might notice that some responses to questions are met with derisive comments. Don't let Internet know-it-alls get you down. Take time to read the Frequently Asked Questions (FAQs) available for most newsgroups, so that you don't ask a question that's been answered many times before. Here's a Web site that lists the FAQs for most newsgroups: **www.faqs.org**. If you don't see the FAQs there, let your first message be a post that requests the location of the FAQs. Someone will point you in the right direction. Most questions are answered the same day they are posted.

Newsgroup management

Ready to see if newsgroups are for you? All you need is an Internet connection and a Web browser, such as Internet Explorer, which is bundled free with every PC. Open your Web browser, and try Google Groups. If you're not sure where to begin, you can type in words that describe what you want to know. Google finds specific messages that contain those words and points you to one or more newsgroups that have the words you entered. You can choose to view all the messages in the newsgroup or just read a specific message that matches your search.

To post your own message via Google, or a follow-up message to one you've read, you first need to sign up for a free account. Once you fill in the registration form, proceed accordingly. First, click the "Post a new message" link from the main newsgroup page, or when viewing someone else's message, click "Post a follow-up to this message". Then, type up your message. If you want to see your message before you send it, click the "Preview message" button. Or click the "Post message no preview button", if you're all set.

FIRST PERSON INSIGHTS
Virtual soulmates

Ellen is one of my best friends, yet I have never met her face-to-face! Actually, I don't even know what her voice sounds like! She and I met online in a fibromyalgia chat room. When I first received the diagnosis, I spent a lot of late nights online, looking for information on treatments, research . . . anything. Instead, I found a friend! At first, we talked a lot in a public chat area about fibro in general. As we got to know each other better, we began exchanging private e-mails on a pretty regular basis.

Ellen has helped me to keep calm and take one day at a time. This kind of advice was so needed in the beginning stages, when I was totally overwhelmed. How would I ever cope with a job and a busy household with a husband, two kids and a dog? I was so tired. And so scared. Ellen's been there. Her fibromyalgia was diagnosed a few years ago. She also has a couple of kids and a busy life. She understands how suffocating it can feel when you realize that this condition isn't going to go away. She has given me tips on practical matters, like resting up in the evenings and learning to say no and mean it when I'm asked to volunteer in the kids' school. She's also encouraged me to be more assertive with my doctor. Ellen lives in Oklahoma, and I'm not sure we will ever meet in person. For now, I'm grateful for her kindness, caring, and wisdom. I am so glad she and I had the chance to connect, thanks to the magic of the Internet.

—Monica T., Clearwater, AZ

Helpful resources

After Any Diagnosis
by Carol Svec

The Health Resource
You don't have to search the Internet yourself. There are a number of companies that offer this service for a fee. One such company, called the Health Resource, will do extensive Internet research compilation that is customized to your diagnosis. The company's Internet specialists will comb through the Internet and other sources and locate medical articles geared toward your specific situation, including mainstream, experimental, and alternative treatments, along with top specialists. In a week to 10 days, you will receive a hard copy of their findings in a bound booklet, complete with glossary. Prices range from $150 to $400.
800-949-0090
www.theheathresource.com

Your Support Team

Creating a health team
take charge of your health

You may not feel up to taking an active, ongoing role in making decisions about your fibromyalgia. But you can't ask your family physician to manage all aspects of it. Even if you were raised in an era when a doctor's word was not questioned, you need to start regarding your physician as a consultant, a member of the "team" that is helping you to manage your condition. You'll need to pull in other health care professionals, especially if you want to explore other treatment options and hope to make lifestyle and dietary changes.

The best way to accomplish this is by assembling a team of people who will help you manage your fibromyalgia. This team can range from a rheumatologist (see page 102) to a physiatrist (see page 104). Bear in mind that you're seeking professionals with similar values and philosophies about fibromyalgia. You need to feel comfortable with them and confident in their ability to treat you, and they need to be willing to listen to your input. Remember, the more input from you, the more likely you are to see positive results in your treatment.

Creating a partnership

Developing a good relationship with your primary care doctor requires effort on both sides. Just as you have rights and responsibilities as a patient, your doctor has certain rights and responsibilities. And as with any relationship, the doctor-patient one rests on respect and trust. It's a partnership. These are some of your rights in the doctor-patient relationship:

◆ To be fully informed about your diagnosis, prognosis, and treatment

◆ To have a say in decisions affecting your health

◆ To have all your questions and concerns dealt with

◆ To have your medical records released only with your consent

◆ To have reasonable access to your doctor

◆ To be told about the costs and risks of treatment

◆ To change doctors, request a referral, or get a second opinion

◆ To be seen within a reasonable amount of time

◆ To be told about how a test or procedure works, how much it costs, and what the alternatives and risks are before consenting to treatment

In return, doctors have a right to be treated with courtesy, to be allowed enough time to make a diagnosis, to have their advice followed carefully, and to be notified in a timely manner if you must cancel or change an appointment.

Your primary care doctor
know what you want from your GP

If your condition has been accurately diagnosed and you are happy with your current primary care doctor, then by all means stick with this doctor. Even after you have been referred to a specialist, you will still need to have a regular doctor on hand. Just because you have fibromyalgia does not mean you will be spared an occasional bout with the flu or a sinus infection. A good primary care physician should act as the "gatekeeper" who manages your general health care and knows when to send you on to a more specialized doctor. Most primary care doctors are generalists, so they usually take a "symptom-by-symptom" approach to treating complaints. Moreover, they can only rely on the information they get from their patients. Most patients don't know how to articulate their symptoms, so the doctor often gets incomplete or misleading information. This is especially true of fibromyalgia. Undoubtedly, some doctors are more familiar with treating fibromyalgia and more effective at it than others. Likewise, some are more compassionate. Then again, an ideal doctor is very much a matter of personal taste. While some patients prefer a straightforward, cut-and-dried approach, others favor a more sympathetic bedside manner.

When Should You Get a Second Opinion?

There are several instances in which you are justified in seeking a second opinion: if the diagnosis is uncertain or life-threatening; if the tests or treatment are controversial, experimental, or risky; if you do not like the doctor's approach; if you have questions about the doctor's competence. Do not be afraid that by asking for a second opinion you are offending your doctor. Most doctors want their patients to be proactive about their care and are more than happy to recommend other specialists for them to see. Remember, though, that a number of health insurers don't pay for a second opinion, so ask beforehand whether your insurer will.

Tips for choosing a Primary Care Physician

If you move to a new town or take a new job with a different health insurance company or HMO than your previous employer used, you will find yourself shopping for a new doctor to entrust with this crucial new factor in your life.

How to find a new doctor:

◆ Start with your former doctor. Chances are he or she will probably know someone to refer you to.

◆ Call the local hospital and see if it has a doctor on staff experienced in treating fibromyalgia.

◆ Call your local hospital's referral line. It will refer you to doctors in the area who are taking on new patients.

When you find a doctor who can treat your fibromyalgia, ask if you can do an initial interview to see if you're a good match. Ask before you go whether the physician charges a fee for this appointment.

Remember that under the Health Insurance Portability and Accountability Act that took effect in April 2003, you have the right to a copy of your medical records. Before you switch doctors, get a copy and correct any errors. Make several duplicates to give to your new primary care physician and other doctors you may be seeing. Be sure to add the corrected records to your health journal (see pages 16–17).

Your rheumatologist
your first line of defense

Chances are it was a rheumatologist who finally gave you the diagnosis of fibromyalgia. That's because a rheumatologist is specially trained to uncover the causes of mysterious muscle pain. A rheumatologist is an internist who has additional training and experience in diagnosing and treating arthritis and other diseases of the muscles, joints, and bones, including fibromyalgia. After completing four years of medical school and three years of training in either internal medicine or pediatrics, rheumatologists then spend another two to three years in specialty training. Most rheumatologists who intend to treat patients usually become board-certified. After they have completed training, they must then pass a rigorous exam conducted by the American Board of Internal Medicine to become certified.

Questions to Ask Specialists

Bear in mind, it's rare that you will speak to the doctor before your first appointment. However, his or her staff should be able to answer these simple questions:

How long has the doctor been specializing in fibromyalgia? Some rheumatologists specialize in other disorders, such as lupus or arthritis, and do very little work with fibromyalgia patients. Some may not specialize in any one disease.

How much does the doctor charge for a consultation? Does his or her office accept your insurance?

What type of information does the doctor need to see on that first consultation? Ask if it should be sent in advance of the appointment. Having the right information on hand can make or break a visit with a specialist. Be sure you have exactly what the doctor will need to best evaluate your case (see pages 118–119).

I've been in a lot of pain for a long time with my fibromyalgia. Even so, it's hard to find the exact words to describe my pain to my doctor. I'm even a little embarrassed about how much I hurt.

As if it's not enough to simply hurt, there's also the matter of feeling bad about it, or feeling as if it's a sign of personal weakness. Rest assured that others feel as you do. Remember, we're not a society that's comfortable with pain. As for dealing with your doctor, keep these tips in mind at your next appointment:

◆ Point out precisely where it hurts. Does your pain stay in one place, or does it move around? Tell the doctor.

◆ On a scale of zero to 10, zero meaning no pain, and 10 meaning the worst imaginable pain, describe how much you hurt. In the last week, what was the highest level of pain you felt? Where did you feel it? When did it hurt the least? How badly does it hurt right now?

◆ Describe what makes your pain better or worse. Does it hurt more when you move in certain ways?

◆ Use specific words like *sharp, stabbing, dull, aching, burning, shock-like, tingling, throbbing,* and *pressing.*

◆ Explain also how the pain affects your daily life—does it impact your sleep? Work? How is your mood? Are you sad? Cranky?

◆ Talk about past treatments, too. Have you tried yoga, massage, or hot and cold therapy? Have you taken over-the-counter medicines? What about supplements or herbal remedies?

Your physiatrist
help for muscle pain

A physiatrist (pronounced "fizz-ee-at-trist") is a medical doctor who has specialized in physical medicine and rehabilitation. Physiatrists can treat a variety of problems, from sore knees to spinal cord injuries. They treat patients from all age groups and impact upon all the major bodily systems. For example, a physiatrist would treat a child with a sports injury, an elderly woman with a broken hip, or a knitter who has carpal tunnel syndrome. Their objective is restoring function to people who are impaired or limited. They also treat chronic pain, such as the muscular aches and soreness you are experiencing from your fibromyalgia.

To become a physiatrist, a doctor must complete three or more years of training in physical medicine and rehabilitation. To become board-certified in physical medicine and rehabilitation, physiatrists must pass both written and oral exams administered by the American Board of Physical Medicine and Rehabilitation.

Physiatrists typically offer a nonsurgical approach to pain and injury. Before beginning treatment, they will perform a thorough history and a physical exam to find the source of your pain, even when a standard test doesn't reveal a specific problem.

Specifically, a physiatrist may prescribe drugs or assistive devices, such as a brace or an artificial limb. They also use diverse therapies such as heat and cold, electrotherapies, massage, biofeedback, traction, and therapeutic exercises.

ASK THE EXPERTS

Where can I find a physiatrist near me?

You can start by contacting your local hospitals or medical centers for a referral. You may want to explain to the person fielding your call that your key issue is fibromyalgia. They may be able to link you to a physiatrist experienced with the syndrome. You can also check with the American Academy of Physical Medicine and Rehabilitation. It has a complete listing of board-certified physiatrists practicing in the U.S. You can reach them by phone: 312-464-9700. Or check our their Web site at **www.aapmr.org**.

How does a physical therapist differ from a physiatrist?

Unlike a physiatrist, a physical therapist, or PT, is not a medical doctor, but a highly trained, skilled individual who will work with you to develop a hands-on physical program to treat your fibromyalgia. These therapies may include heat and cold and electrical therapy, as well as hydrotherapy, to temporarily relieve your pain and reduce muscle spasms, ultimately preparing you for exercise and activity.

A PT may also teach you to perform practical activities more safely and efficiently, such as getting out of bed and into a chair, or getting into a car or aboard a bus. A PT will also prescribe exercises to improve your muscle strength, joint mobility, and cardiovascular function. To find a PT in your area, contact the American Physical Therapy Association at **www.apta.org** or call them at 703-684-2782.

Pain specialists
a new speciality that can help

Depending upon the severity of your fibromyalgia, your geographic location, and what your health insurance allows, you may want a pain specialist to be involved in your care. While there is as yet no one specialty for those physicians who focus on treating pain, many doctors from many different disciplines can become certified in pain medicine.

The practice of pain medicine is multidisciplinary in its approach, incorporating methods from various specialties to ensure that a patient in pain is properly evaluated and treated. A doctor who chooses to become certified in this field may already be an anesthesiologist, an internist, a neurologist, an orthopedic surgeon, a physiatrist, or even a psychiatrist. Pain management specialists believe that integrating all these specialties is crucial in properly treating your pain, regardless of whether you are suffering from a ruptured disk, a headache, or the persistent aches of fibromyalgia.

Pain medicine specialists use a broad-based approach to treat all pain-based disorders, ranging from pain as a symptom of disease to pain as the primary disease. In other words, a pain expert may use many different approaches—be it surgery, medicine, or a course of physical therapy—to help you best manage your pain. The American Academy of Pain Medicine (AAPM) has evolved as the primary organization for doctors practicing in this specialty in the U.S. To locate a pain specialist, go first to their Web site, **www.painmed.org**, or call them at 847-375-4731. You can also contact your local hospital and ask for a referral, always mentioning your fibromyalgia.

ASK THE EXPERTS

Doesn't my primary care doctor know how to treat my pain?

It is not reasonable to expect every physician or health professional to handle all aspects of your care. A primary care doctor is there to help manage your whole health team, including pain specialists.

How do I go about describing the quality of my pain, as my doctor requests?

Talking about pain can be difficult. To help your doctor better understand your situation, try thinking about your pain as a separate entity that you can track. Ask yourself: When did the pain start? What provokes it? What does it feel like? Does it travel? Where do you feel it? When do you get it? What helps lessen it?

Your pharmacist
the "safety net" in managing your illness

Because you will probably be taking many different medications to help alleviate your fibromyalgia symptoms, it is a good idea to develop a relationship with your pharmacist. This way, your pharmacist can act as a "safety net" in managing your prescriptions, not only for your fibromyalgia medicine but for any possible adverse drug interactions with other medications you may take as well.

That's why the best strategy is to work with one pharmacist—someone whose experience and background you trust and who takes the time to answer your questions. Also, using one pharmacist and pharmacy will make it easier to keep your medication records up-to-date. If you use the more impersonal drug chains for your pharmaceutical needs, then make sure to do a drug check with your doctor at least once a year. That's where you bring in the actual bottles of your prescription medication and check that each one is still correct.

Always double-check with your pharmacist about when and how to take your medications, and make sure these instructions match what is printed on the bottle.

Keep It Handy

Always keep a list in your wallet or purse of the medicines you are taking and the dosages. In case of an emergency, this list will prove invaluable.

ASK THE EXPERTS

I've found a couple of online pharmacies that sell my analgesic medication for half the price. Is it okay to use them?

While some online pharmacies are reputable, watch out for sham pharmacies that sell expired or illegal medication. Beware of sites that do not require you to send in your doctor's prescription and do not guarantee their medications up until their expiration date. The best way to find a trustworthy online pharmacy is to ask your doctor for a recommendation. While it may cost you more money, it's a better idea to develop an ongoing relationship with an actual pharmacist, who is more likely to do a better job managing all your medications.

My pharmacist said I should try generic pain medication to save money, but my doctor won't prescribe it. Why not?

Some doctors believe that there are subtle differences between the generic and the brand-name medications, even though studies have shown that brand-name medication is not necessarily more effective than generic medication. Again, talk to your doctor about it. If you need to save money on your medicine, then your doctor should try to accommodate your situation.

Your advocate
we all need someone to lean on

As you build your health care team, do not forget one of the most important elements: your personal advocate, or coach. This should be a friend or family member who can help you navigate the halls of medicine. Your coach can be your spouse, partner, relative, or good friend—basically, someone who will stand by your side and be an advocate for you when you need one. Your coach should be open-minded, a good listener, and, above all, someone who respects your confidences.

Your coach should be willing to be a sounding board for the emotional ups and downs you are likely to face and also be willing to pitch in on practical matters, such as going with you to doctor's appointments or running errands when you are too tired to move. It may seem a lot to ask of someone, but most people like helping others out. And who knows? Someday you may be able to return the favor. A good coach, or advocate, is someone who:

- Stays informed about your illness, symptoms, and medications.

- Keeps up-to-date about new treatments and advances.

- Accompanies you on doctor's visits if you wish and speaks up for you when you feel the doctor doesn't understand what you're trying to say.

- Takes notes on what the doctor or other health professional tells you after an examination, allowing you to focus entirely on listening.

- Helps you to keep track of medications and generally encourages you to continue the healthy habits you are struggling to maintain.

- Is willing to deal with paperwork and make calls on your behalf.

- Can share a good joke with you.

Some people appoint their spouse as coach. Others prefer someone with a little more distance—a cousin or a good friend. Some of the best advocates are those who have also suffered from the same condition as you or have loved ones struggling with it. If you do not know anyone willing to commit to being your coach, you might try joining a support group or online forum, where you will be able to get advice and support from others in the same boat.

Another key role your advocate should play is acting as your exercise pal. Because exercise is so helpful to people with fibromyalgia and so hard to maintain, enlist the support of your advocate in your goals. Plan to meet at the gym a few times a week or, for example, at the pool every Tuesday after work. Working out with a buddy is a great motivation to stick with your exercise program.

Using your health journal
good information at your fingertips

While it's true that living with a chronic disease has changed your life, you can do a lot to keep those changes minimal. In fact, with some smart planning and a little knowledge, you can learn to manage your fibromyalgia like a pro. Some even say that learning how to manage their illness taught them invaluable life lessons. So how do you manage a chronic illness? Take a tip from the CEOs of the business world—besides a good team, you need good information.

Your good information is right at your fingertips. Literally. All you need to do is pay attention to your body and track your symptoms in your health journal. Before a doctor's visit, read through the last three months and see if there are any new patterns developing.

Keep track of things, preferably on a daily basis—from flare-ups and when they happen to days when you feel good and why. Was it the acupuncture treatment, the massage, or the water aerobics class you just took? What about the days in which you feel particularly lousy? Is it because you skipped a dose of your pain meds or is it the result of a stressful event in your life—your son's graduation and the party you threw, or the recent round of firings at work?

One key thing to keep tabs on is your pain. You should have a special section in your journal for pain diary entries. Here you note down the type and degree of pain you are experiencing. You should also keep a log of pain medications you are taking, noting their effectiveness and any side effects.

Looking for patterns

From time to time, it's a good idea to review your health journal. You are looking for any unusual occurrence, as well as any patterns. Again, it's important to bear in mind that it takes time to learn to pay attention to your body. Reviewing your journal will keep you in the habit of thinking about your health. Things to look for:

◆ Changes in sleep patterns. Are you sleeping more or less? Is your sleep restful or fitful?

◆ Changes in pain. Is your pain worsening or lessening? Are there any precipitating factors that make the pain worse or better? Is it worse or better at various times of the day? How are you handling it? Is it impacting any daily activities?

◆ Diet and digestion patterns. Are you craving any foods? Having difficulty digesting certain foods? Eating more or less? At different times of the day?

◆ Accounts of any life events that seem to be affecting your health, plus a record of your daily stress level.

◆ Emotional or mood patterns. This one is hard. You are looking for patterns of feelings; for example, feelings of sadness striking every afternoon may reveal a blood-sugar problem entirely separate from your fibromyalgia.

Preparing for an appointment
get organized for your next doctor's appointment

Given the number of doctors you no doubt have already seen, you may feel that your medical life with all its tests, prescriptions, and insurance forms is consuming all your time and energy. It doesn't have to be that way. Start thinking of your doctor's appointments as business meetings, and prepare accordingly. In other words, think of yourself as a professional who has an agenda with clear goals. Here are some steps to take that will take some of the stress out of your next appointment:

◆ Figure out three key things you want to accomplish and write them down. Similarly, write down all your questions in order of priority. Be realistic and realize that your doctor may have time to answer only a few during a visit.

◆ Review your health journal and pain diary since your last visit. Jot down any improvements or changes you may be experiencing. If you are seeing your doctor to review your medication, you might want to bring in the bottles to show the doctor; this is especially important if you are seeing more than one doctor.

◆ Have photocopies of any pertinent test results that you can give your doctor to keep in your file. (Don't give your original test results.)

◆ Note any complementary or alternative treatments you may be trying. It's important that you keep the doctor in the loop.

◆ If you're visiting a new doctor, make sure you have arranged to have all your medical records and copies of your test results transferred from your previous doctor.

During the appointment

- Be crisp. Don't get involved in pleasantries. Your doctor has only a limited number of minutes with you. Use them well.

- Give the doctor a brief overview of how you've been since your last appointment, not just how you've been feeling the last few days or so.

- Ask your most important questions first and be as concise as possible. Many patients try to discuss a lengthy laundry list that can't possibly be covered in a single visit.

- Explain to the doctor the main reason for your visit today (don't be afraid to refer to your notes) and what you'd like him or her to do for you.

- Using the lists you've compiled beforehand, give the doctor an honest report about your concerns, problems you may be having with treatments, results of visits to other health professionals and the outcome of self-help treatments you've tried.

- If you are not absolutely clear about the following basic information, try to get it at this appointment: your diagnosis and how the condition affects you; the purpose, risks, and results of tests; when to call the doctor about the side effects of a medication or lack of response to one; treatment choices, including the benefits and side effects of each. Ask when and how best to contact the doctor.

Working with a therapist
it's okay to admit you're not okay

Having a chronic illness like fibromyalgia can be a huge, life-changing event, not only for you, but for your family. It's natural for you to feel anxious, sad, angry, and yes, utterly confused. Mental health professionals know how overwhelming this time in your life can be. "Don't wait until you are seriously depressed," cautions Elizabeth Clark, Ph.D., C.S.W., executive director of the National Association of Social Workers and an expert in chronic illness. "All too often people don't seek out support when they need it. The message we get from society. too, is to 'buck up!' After all, it's 'only' a chronic illness!"

If you think that once you start a course of counseling or psychotherapy it will be ongoing and last for years, think again. Clark explains that short-term treatment can be immensely helpful for someone like you. (See pages 58–59 for more on cognitive-behavioral therapy that requires only 16 sessions.)

Psychotherapists can be psychologists with a master's or Ph.D. or social workers who have a master's degree in social work (M.S.W.). Some social workers have gone on for additional training. Those who have gotten a doctorate in mental health are Ph.D.s. Note: Psychotherapists cannot prescribe medications; psychiatrists, medical doctors who specialize in mental disorders, can prescribe medication.

Before you visit a therapist, take a close look at your health journal and pain diary. Check for any major trends or changes in your emotional or mental state. Do your best to articulate these issues to the therapist, who will then be in a better position to work with you on these problems and help you repair any relationships negatively influenced by your illness.

Talking it out

When I finally got my diagnosis of fibromyalgia four years ago, I thought I was on my way to recovery. Wrong. It has taken another two years to find the right medications that work for me. There were months of trial and error. It was just awful. Not surprisingly, I found myself getting really depressed. I felt that my life as I knew it was over. It was so unfair. My sister finally got me to see a therapist. I didn't want to. I had seen enough doctors. But she was different. She listened. And she picked up on my anger. That was the real problem. I was so angry at this disease that I couldn't think straight. She showed me that being angry was causing a lot more harm than good. What really turned me around was when she said that suffering was part of life. No one gets a free ride. She was right.

—*Babe S., Bedford ND*

Joining a support group
sharing your experience with others

Having fibromyalgia can make you feel set apart from your family and friends. It can also feel as if no one else can possibly understand what it's like to live with this day in and day out—not even your spouse or coach. But you are wrong. There are several national organizations filled with people who share your situation. They draw strength from each other during their weekly support meetings or online through e-mail. They also play a very important role in treating fibromyalgia by disseminating the latest research results, pushing for new legislation regarding medication and drug companies, and advocating for fibromyalgia patients who may feel overlooked by their doctors.

Even more important, a fibromyalgia support group can serve as a sounding board when you are having a particularly bad day—and they can help you put your suffering in perspective. Plus, there will probably be at least one person in your group who has gone through experiences very similar to yours and may be able to provide valuable insight and emotional support.

Where do you begin and how do you find a group targeted to people like yourself? If you are seeing a specialist who deals a lot with fibromyalgia patients, he or she may have a list of groups meeting in your area. Local hospitals may sponsor support groups, including one geared to either fibromyalgia patients or those with chronic pain. It's worth a call to the hospital's community relations department to find out when and where a local group meets. Some are free. If the group is run by a trained therapist, there may be a fee to join.

ASK THE EXPERTS

I'd like to try a fibromyalgia support group. But I am nervous—what do they discuss, and do I have to confess everything about myself and my fibromyalgia?

Breaking into any new group for the first time can be unnerving. And no, you certainly don't have to reveal any more than you feel comfortable revealing. In fact, in some support and discussion groups, it's perfectly fine to sit and listen, with no pressure to participate.

As for the topic, it depends on the group. Some are structured and choose a topic in advance—whether it's a controversial new treatment or learning ways to cut back in your life and say no. Other groups are more free-flowing, with individual members reporting on their progress and the discussion evolving from there.

It's a good idea to sit in on a group at least once before deciding if it's right for you.

Where can I find out about support groups?

Go online and contact the American Chronic Pain Association. Their e-mail address is **acpa@pacbell.net**.

Helpful resources

**National Association of
Social Workers**
750 First Street NE, Suite 700
Washington, DC, 20002
Clinical social workers are the
nation's largest providers of mental
health and therapy services, out-
numbering both psychologists and
psychiatrists. They provide mental
health services in urban and rural
settings, where they may be the only
licensed provider of mental health
services available.
202-408-8600
www.socialworkers.org

**National Mental Health
Association**
The oldest and largest nonprofit
organization addressing all aspects
of mental health, with more than
340 affiliates nationwide. Their
resource center provides referrals to
local treatment centers and lists of
mental health providers.
800-969-6642
www.nmha.org

CHAPTER 8

The Role of Nutrition

Principles of good nutrition
what constitutes a healthy diet?

Having a chronic illness often causes people to reassess their eating habits. That can be a blessing, especially if your diet was not the greatest before your diagnosis. Learning how to eat well can not only help you feel better but also give you back some control over your health. The question then is, what constitutes a healthy diet? If you follow the headlines, you may be confused over how to eat right. High protein or high carbohydrate? Low-fat or high-fat? Unlimited fruit or no fruit?

Fortunately, the fundamentals of healthy eating are constant and quite simple to master. The right foods can power your brain, fend off infections, and strengthen your muscles. By eating right you help shrink cholesterol, blood-sugar, and blood-pressure levels. And when your body has the food and nutrients it needs, you are less likely to be haunted by food cravings.

Keeping to a healthy diet is actually pretty straightforward. You need to eat a wide variety of fresh foods to ensure that you get the proper amounts of nutrients and vitamins. And you need to watch your portion size. Proper serving size is most important to healthy eating. Many of us eat portions that are too big and supply too many calories. Portion sizes of packaged, take-out, and restaurant foods are often larger than necessary and filled with too many calories. It's no wonder so many Americans are overweight. A registered dietitian (see pages 128–129) or a weight-management program can offer you an individualized eating plan.

ASK THE EXPERTS

Ever since my fibromyalgia set in I have been gaining weight. I am so upset about my weight gain, I am ready to try just about anything. I heard about a weight-loss program that guarantees that I'll lose five pounds a week. Is that healthy?

Be wary of programs that promise dramatic weight loss. Weight loss should be slow and steady—no more than one to two pounds a week. A goal of slow weight loss gives you more time to change your eating habits, and weight lost slowly may be easier to keep off. Much of the weight lost quickly is water weight, which is quick to come back. Steer clear of programs that blame weight gain on particular types of foods and tell you to eliminate entire food groups—for example, grain products. Grain foods supply fiber and other important nutrients that are tough to replace with other foods.

Metabolism

Metabolism is the total energy used by your body for all its processes. It has two components—catabolism (breaking down substances) and anabolism (storing energy). Your "metabolic rate" is the number of calories your body burns in a 24-hour day to fuel basic body functions, including digestion of food and physical activity.

The right stuff
there's plenty to choose from

There are simple, basic guidelines for maintaining a balanced diet that will help you to feel better, stave off chronic diseases such as some cancers and heart disease, and help you manage your fibromyalgia. They may not be new, but you have never before had a more compelling reason to follow them.

Eat a variety of foods

That means eating more whole grains, fruits, and vegetables than most Americans do. A healthy diet includes choices from each of the five different food groups: breads and cereals, fruits, vegetables, dairy products, and meats.

Cut down on fat and cholesterol

The American Heart Association (AHA) recommends that people limit fat intake to 30 percent of their daily calories. For someone who eats 2,000 calories per day, this would mean eating 67 grams or less of fat daily and 300 milligrams of cholesterol a day, which equals about one-and-a-half eggs.

Eat vegetables, fruits, and whole grains

They supply the carbohydrates that are the basic energy source for our bodies. Carbohydrates in general should make up 55 to 60 percent of your calories. But not all carbohydrates are created equal. Simple carbohydrates, such as refined sugar and honey, have few other nutrients. You'll get a quick (but short-lived) energy boost from a candy bar, but not much else. You digest it quickly, which drives up your blood sugar but strains your insulin-producing pancreas. Complex carbohydrates, on the other hand--fruits, vegetables, and whole grain products, like high-fiber bread—are digested more slowly, are lower in fat, and create a sensation of fullness. If you eat a piece of whole-wheat bread, for example, you'll get energy, but also vitamins, minerals, fiber, and some protein. Some types of fiber can keep you from becoming constipated; they result in softer stools and more rapid elimination.

Keep sugar and salt to a minimum

Sugar, which adds empty, extra calories, can add to weight gain and to tooth decay. When you check a food label for sugar, look for the words *sucrose, fructose, honey,* and *dextrin.* Sodium causes your body to retain water, making you feel bloated and uncomfortable; it can adversely affect your blood pressure.

Most Americans consume more than three teaspoons (8,000 milligrams, or 8 grams) of salt each day. Most of that salt comes not from salt shakers but from processed foods. Check food labels. If you see the word *salt, soda,* or *sodium* high up in the ingredient list, then the product contains high amounts of sodium. Dietitians, the U.S. Department of Health and Human Services, and the American Heart Association all recommend limiting your daily salt intake to half a teaspoon (2,400 milligrams).

The Perimeter Diet

Here is an easy diet to follow: Shop the perimeters of the store. Next time you're buying groceries, note the layout of the supermarket. You will notice that most of the goods in the middle are refined, processed items that you can live without. Stick to the items displayed along the edges or perimeter of the store—these are typically the produce and dairy aisles.

Portion control
watch those serving sizes

The key to healthy eating lies in portion control. The U.S. Department of Agriculture's Food Guide Pyramid recommends a range of servings per day from each food group. If you are trying to lose weight, start with the lowest number of servings recommended.

Include grain foods like bread, cereal, pasta, and rice. Why? Your body needs these grain foods for their carbohydrates, the body's top energy source. Grains also supply important minerals and B vitamins. To get enough fiber, choose whole grains whenever possible; for example, a whole-grain cereal at breakfast and a whole-wheat bread sandwich for lunch.

Eat: 6 to 11 servings daily (each meal may have more than one serving)

Food	Serving Size	Common Measure
Bagel	1/2 small	1/2 packaged English muffin
Bread, toast	1 slice	Slice from standard loaf
Breakfast cereal	1 cup	Standard teacup
Pasta or rice	1/2 cup cooked	Cupped palm

Include fruits and vegetables. Why? Fruits and vegetables dish up vitamins A and C, fiber, and a slew of natural compounds that are good for overall health. They are also filling and relatively low in calories.

Eat: 2 to 4 servings of fruit and 3 to 5 servings (or more) of vegetables daily

Food	Serving Size	Common Measure
Fruit	1 medium	Baseball
Fruit juice	6 fluid ounces	Juice glass
Vegetables	1/2 cup	Bulb portion of lightbulb

Include dairy products. Why? Dairy products like milk and yogurt supply calcium, the mineral necessary to build strong bones. Calcium is particularly important for those at high risk of osteoporosis—older women and people with hyperthyroidism. Cheese also supplies calcium but is higher in fat and calories. To control calories, choose reduced-fat cheese, along with low-fat or nonfat milk and yogurt. Try calcium-fortified juice or soy milk if you do not use dairy products.

Eat: 2 to 3 servings daily

Food	Serving Size	Common Measure
Cheese	1 ounce	2 dominoes
Milk, yogurt	1 cup	Yogurt container
Fortified juice	1 cup	Yogurt container

Include a variety of proteins. Why? Meat, poultry, fish, beans, eggs, and nuts all supply protein, the nutrient your body needs to build and repair muscle and tissue. Each also offers its own unique benefits; for example, meat is high in iron and zinc, fish supplies omega-3 fatty acids, and beans have fiber. The Food Guide Pyramid recommends relatively small portions.

Eat: 2 servings daily

Food	Serving Size	Common Measure
Beans (kidney, pinto, etc.)	1/2 cup (replaces 1 ounce meat)	Bulb portion of lightbulb
Eggs	1 (replaces 1 ounce meat)	Large egg
Meat, chicken, fish	3 ounces	Palm of a woman's hand
Peanut butter	2 tablespoons	1 walnut (in shell)

Finding nutritional help
diet professionals can make all the difference

Try as you might, it can be hard to find a diet that works for you. This is especially true if you also have symptoms of irritable bowel syndrome (see pages 70–71). Don't be discouraged. Instead seek out some professional support. The best person to seek out is a registered dietitian. She can teach you about the basics of healthful eating and about making specific changes in your diet for fibromyalgia and other health issues you may have.

At your first appointment, a registered dietitian will review your medical history, ask you questions about your current diet, and plan changes to your eating habits that are appropriate for your illness. Follow-up appointments will review your progress and adjust your diet as needed for your condition. Consultation with a registered dietitian (or R.D.) for medical purposes is covered by some, but not all, insurance plans, so check with your insurance company regarding coverage.

Pyramid Power

Look on the back of most cereal boxes, and you're likely to find a familiar sketch of the Food Guide Pyramid put out by the U.S. Department of Agriculture. Choose most of your foods from the bottom two layers of the pyramid and fewer from the top, based on the recommended number of daily servings. That will guide you to a balanced diet with moderate amounts of sugar, sodium, and saturated fat, and with the proper amount of calories to maintain a healthy weight.

ASK THE EXPERTS

What is the difference between a nutritionist and a registered dietitian?

A nutritionist has studied nutrition and often has received a master's degree. Registered dietitians are health professionals who have completed an accredited education and training program and have passed a national credentialing exam. Many registered dietitians also have master's degrees in nutrition.

How do I find a dietitian?

You can find a dietitian on your own through the Yellow Pages or by contacting the American Dietetic Association at 800-877-1600, ext. 5000, or at **www.eatright.org**.

Smart Tips to Cut Calories

1. Enhance the amount of meat you eat by tenderizing it before cooking. Tenderizing (pounding with a mallet) makes a little bit of meat look bigger. It also makes it cook faster and makes it quicker to freeze and to thaw.

2. "Oven-fry" instead of pan- or deep-frying. You'll get crisp, moist, flavorful foods with very little fat. Lightly coat the breaded food with cooking spray and cook in a very hot oven (450°F to 500°F) for five to seven minutes, depending on thickness.

3. Use cooking spray whenever possible. Coating a nonstick skillet or wok with cooking spray rather than tablespoons of oil saves hundreds of fat calories in stir-fries and sautés. Add a little broth halfway through sautéing; this creates steam that helps cook vegetables to a tender crisp.

4. Roast fresh vegetables to concentrate their flavor. (It's a nice alternative to steamed vegetables.) If you're cooking for a few people, just toss the cut vegetables with a little olive oil and seasoning, spread on a baking sheet, and bake in a hot oven (450°) for 20 to 30 minutes.

5. Use cornstarch to thicken sauces instead of cream or flour. One tablespoon of cornstarch thickens one cup of liquid to the consistency of pancake syrup. The liquid must be brought to a boil to achieve its maximum thickness. Cornstarch is twice as powerful a thickener as flour, so you will use half as much. It adds far fewer calories than thickening with butter or cream.

The elimination diet
Sometimes, it's what you don't eat

Could something you are eating make you feel worse? If your instinct tells you that something in your diet is adding to your woes, possibly even triggering your symptoms, you can determine what this is by temporarily adopting an elimination diet. Start by eliminating all the classic irritating foods and beverages (see list on opposite page). Wait a few days. Then, one by one, add back foods or groups of foods—say, cheeses—and keep a food diary to record any reactions. Wait at least two days before adding new foods to your diet. Strict elimination diets are not balanced nutritionally and should not be followed for long periods of time.

A food journal is essential for figuring out which foods, if any, are contributing to your symptoms. You don't need to buy a notebook—instead, make your own journal pages by hand or on the computer. Keep them simple and easy to carry with you during the day. Maintain your food diary for at least a week and for as long as you are working with the elimination diet and reintroduction of foods.

Each journal page should have room for the following columns:

- Date

- Meal and time of day

- What you ate and drank, being as specific as possible and including cooking method and condiments

- How much you ate

- What you were doing while eating

Foods to Consider Eliminating:

Alcohol and vinegar
Red wine, champagne, beer, dark-colored liquors; balsamic or red-wine vinegar.

Caffeine-containing beverages and foods
Regular coffee, tea, iced tea, and cola; other caffeine-containing soft drinks; chocolate.

Aspartame *(Nutrasweet)* An artificial sweetener found in some diet drinks.

Yeast
Fresh-baked, yeast-risen bread products.

Dairy products
All cheeses except American, cream, and cottage cheese; cheese-containing foods, such as pizza; yogurt, sour cream.

Certain fruits and vegetables
Citrus fruits (orange, grapefruit, lemon, lime) and their juices; raisins and other dried fruit; bananas, red plums, canned figs, avocados, onions and sauerkraut.

Monosodium glutamate (MSG)
Chinese food; many snack foods and prepared foods contain MSG, as do soy products and many soups, broths, and stocks.

Nuts and peanut butter
All nuts and nut butters, including peanut butter.

Nitrates/processed meats
Hot dogs, sausage, bacon, salami, bologna, and other meats that are aged, canned, marinated, or contain nitrates.

Legumes
Broad, lima, fava, and navy beans.

Cooking smart
labor-saving ways to make a meal

After a long day at work, you have neither the energy nor the patience to stand at a sink chopping, cutting, and prepping an elaborate meal. Yet you vowed to make an effort to eat well. It takes a little planning, but you can do it. For instance, instead of chopping and tearing salad ingredients, you can buy bags of ready-made, prewashed salad makings. And you can opt for peeled and washed baby carrots rather than doing the work yourself. Or you can select a healthy, low-fat, low-sodium frozen dinner, and supplement it with a fresh salad or several servings of fruit.

Other shortcuts can save you from slaving over a hot stove, yet still provide a nutrition-packed meal. Here are a few other tips:

◆ Cook earlier in the day if you can, or whenever you are feeling most energized. Reheat the food later.

◆ Cook foods that can be reused, such as a chicken that you can roast, then chop up later for a salad.

◆ Plan small rest breaks when you're preparing food.

◆ Arrange your kitchen for convenience. Keep the most frequently used tools within easy reach.

◆ Sit down. If you can do a task (peeling veggies, for example) more comfortably when you are seated, why stand?

◆ If you must stand, keep a footstool beside you, and place one foot up on the footstool while cooking.

Last woman standing

Now that I had fibromyalgia, standing at the kitchen counter for long periods was just too exhausting. I finally figured out that if my family and I were going to continue to eat well—I needed to sit down. I needed a chair. Not just any chair, mind you, but one with a back and high enough to be level with the counter. This way, I could comfortably sit and chop onions, tomatoes, whatever, and not get tired. Once my husband found me a chair that worked, my fatigue lessened considerably. It's the simple things that can make all the difference.

—Leslie S., Scranton, PA

Helpful resources

American Dietetic Association Complete Food and Nutrition Guide (2nd Edition)
by Roberta Larson Duyff, M.S., R.D., C.F.C.S., American Dietetic Association
Sound advice on eating, including chapters on nutrition and health conditions and on dietary supplements.

Wellness Book of IBS
by Becnel D. Scanlon

American Dietetic Association
Offers nutrition information, including consumer tips, fact sheets, FAQs, resources, and referrals to dietitians.
800 877-1600
www.eatright.org

Fibromyalgia Network
P.O. Box 31750
Tucson, AZ 85751
800-853-2929
www.fmnetnews.com

Complementary Therapies

What to expect
identifying your needs

What therapies will work for you depends on what troubles you most about your fibromyalgia. There are a number of alternative therapies from which to choose, spanning the range from herbs and vitamins to hands-on treatments, such as chiropractic therapy, massage, and acupuncture. Then there are those treatments that focus on the mind-body connection, such as biofeedback and meditation, yoga, and tai chi.

As you explore complementary therapies, be certain to discuss your plans and discoveries with your doctor. It is essential that he knows what you are doing.

FIRST PERSON INSIGHTS

Buyer beware

I have been dealing with fibromyalgia for five years now. The medication helped, but I was getting fed up with the fatigue. I was in a health food store and asked the clerk about herbs to help with fatigue. She showed me about six different herbs that are supposed to help. Well, I bought them all. I tried them for a while, but they didn't do much. I wanted to be in control of my fibromyalgia, but it turned out I was just as ineffective as my doctors. I finally told my doctor what I was doing. He wasn't happy that I did the herbs on my own without telling him. He said there can be adverse herb and drug interactions, as well as adverse reactions with other herbs. We sat in his office and went through everything. He suggested I stick with vitamins and try biofeedback for the pain.

—Dan P., Detroit, MI

◆ **Research what's available.** Support groups can be extremely helpful sources of information. Ask the research librarian at your library
to help you. Do an Internet search using the name of your illness
plus the name of the therapy you want to explore, for example,
fibromyalgia + biofeedback. (For more information on using the
Internet, see Chapter 6).

◆ **Avoid thinking that because something is "natural" it is benign.**
Many of the so-called natural or organic substances touted by alter-
ative healers have not been tested, let alone approved, by the FDA.
Testimonials and anecdotal evidence do not make something safe.
Be especially wary of taking any products or supplements sold
directly by a healer. Talk with your doctor before you try anything.

◆ **Stay alert to how you are feeling.** It's tempting to think that you
feel lousy all the time. In truth, you have good days and bad days.
The more you know about what makes you feel better or worse, the
more you can use that knowledge to improve your well-being.
Review your health journal (see pages 16–17).

◆ **Bear the expense in mind.** Complementary treatments can cost as
much as standard methods—or more, given that many are not covered by insurance plans. Be as frank about your finances as you are
about your physical condition. Some practitioners may be willing to
negotiate their fees.

◆ **Above all, do not fall for the notion that if the therapy fails,
you've failed.** Nothing, not even antibiotics, works equally well for
everyone. Give the new therapy a fair trial—some can take a while to
show a benefit—but if you are not being helped, give it up and try
something else. Or try another person who practices the same therapy; that person may have an insight that makes all the difference.

The complementary approach
look before you leap

In recent years, patient demand has dictated that medicine become less high-tech and more high-touch—and the use of nontraditional treatments has steadily risen. In fact, today even the prestigious National Institutes of Health has recognized the trend with its National Center for Complementary and Alternative Medicine. Among its goals are to find out what treatments actually do provide relief for various diseases.

When used alone, these out-of-the-mainstream treatments are often referred to as alternative. When used in addition to conventional medicine, they are often referred to as complementary. According to the National Institutes of Health, the list of what are considered to be complementary or alternative therapies changes continually as more are proven to be safe and effective and are adopted into conventional health care, and as new approaches to health care emerge.

What will help you depends on what troubles you most about your illness. If you are frightened or angry or depressed, you may benefit from techniques that emphasize the mind-body connection, such as meditation and biofeedback, or exercise that requires mental focus, such as yoga or tai chi. If you decide to explore complementary therapies, be certain to discuss your plans and discoveries with your doctor. It's essential that your doctor knows what you are doing in order to be able to judge how it might interact with your standard treatment.

ASK THE EXPERTS

Where do I find alternative practitioners?

The National Center for Complementary and Alternative Medicine suggests that you contact a professional organization for the type of practitioner you are seeking. Often, these professional organizations provide referrals to practitioners as well as information about the therapy. Professional organizations can be located by searching the Internet or directories in libraries (ask the librarian). One directory is the Directory of Information Resources Online (DIRLINE), compiled by the National Library of Medicine. It contains locations and descriptive information about a variety of alternative health organizations.

What happens if my regular doctor says no to anything alternative?

First, most physicians are recognizing that their patients often seek alternative treatments without informing them. Your doctor will probably be happy that you are even discussing the concept before you plunge ahead. If your doctor says no, without giving you a reason other than that he or she thinks it's all a "bunch of baloney," you will have to weigh that position against your desire to try something new that may or may not help your fibromyalgia and might even harm you. It also depends on what treatment you are seeking. Some of it is baloney; some of it isn't. Chances are good, though, that your physician will respect your desire for a remedy, regardless of where it comes from. Whatever you do, be sure to keep your doctor informed.

Stress management
teaching your mind to soothe your body

You can cope with your fibromyalgia and feel better by using techniques that deal with stress. Practitioners of the so-called mind-body modalities teach you to be more conscious of stress and give you practical things to do about it. It may seem counterintuitive to focus on stress; after all, we're hardwired to recoil from pain and culturally programmed to roll up our sleeves and get on with things. But with proper guidance, stress management techniques can yield enormous benefits, not just physically, but also mentally, emotionally, and spiritually. **Relaxation therapy** encompasses a wide range of techniques designed to reduce stress and tension. Some of the more popular ones are:

Progressive muscle relaxation. You do this by systematically tensing and relaxing the muscles in each part of your body. While sitting comfortably or lying down, inhale and clench your facial muscles, hold the tension for a moment, then exhale and relax those muscles. Do the same thing with your shoulders, one arm, then the other, and so on through your body until you get to your toes. When you're done, stay quietly where you are, and breathe normally for a few minutes.

Guided imagery. The idea here is to imagine a peaceful place and put yourself in the scene. This can be done with a partner who provides the "guidance" by describing the scene, but you can do all the imagining yourself, or listen to a narrated audiotape, soothing music, or environmental sounds, such as birdsong or ocean waves.

Deep breathing. Taking a few minutes each day to practice slow, deep breathing can relieve muscle pain and light-headedness, and improve mental acuity. All you need to do is stand, sit, or lie still. Place your one hand on your belly and slowly inhale until you feel your lungs are full (your belly should expand); then exhale slowly and completely. Repeat that for ten or twelve breaths, and try to do it from time to time throughout the day. Some people find it energizing to do this type of deep breathing before they get out of bed in the morning.

Ask the Experts

Why do people always tell me to breathe deeply whenever I get stressed or upset or angry?

When you get upset, it is usually because something did not go your way or something happened that was out of your control. Either way, the main problem is that you are out of control. One way to counteract that feeling of powerlessness is to do something that you can control, namely, your breathing. By concentrating on your breath and inhaling deeply (your belly should expand) and exhaling slowly, you are not only getting more oxygen into your blood, but also telling yourself that, despite all else, you are in control.

Biofeedback
learning to control the pain

Biofeedback is one of the most effective therapies not only for fibromyalgia but also for the stress of many chronic conditions. And because of its success, many experts don't even consider biofeedback an "alternative approach." It is an integrated component of their treatment plans. The National Institutes of Health considers biofeedback to be mainstream medicine and recommends its greater utilization.

Biofeedback works on the principle that you can be taught to control certain body processes that essentially seem to happen on their own, like heart rate, skin temperature, or even brain waves. To obtain the information—the feedback—that will allow you to learn to change the way your mind/body responds to stress and pain, such as blood-vessel dilation and muscle tension, the biofeedback practitioner uses small sensors, usually placed on the hands, shoulders, or scalp. These sensors are connected to a computer. Depending on which sensors are attached, the computer will transform the information it receives and make it visible or audible via the monitor or speakers. This allows you to see or hear your breath rate, pulse rate, skin temperature and conductance, and even your brain waves, live and in color!

You will then be taught how to breathe more deeply or be asked to visualize a relaxing scene, which will actually influence the sensor readings and thus what you hear or see via the computer. During a training session, you will practice various relaxation techniques while getting continuous feedback from the sensors. Thus, you can see how relaxed breathing can lower your pulse rate or change your brain waves. And you will see how sensitive your body is to stressful thinking. After several sessions, you will be able to consciously exert greater control over your mind/body responses, and see and feel the changes as your hands warm, your muscles relax, your breath slows and deepens, and your mind relaxes.

Why are sensors placed on the hands?

Skin temperature and skin conductance are usually measured on the fingers. The sweat glands and the blood flow through the hands are especially sensitive to stress and emotional reactivity. The stress response lowers peripheral blood flow, which makes hands and feet feel cold— thus the expression "getting cold feet." When you learn how to profoundly relax, your hand temperature will rise and skin conductance will drop. Over time you can learn to sustain a lower level of stress and reactivity throughout the day.

How do you teach your brain to change its waves?

The basic principle in all biofeedback is that once you can perceive something you can begin to change it. The computer makes your brain waves appear before you, linked to a graph or to a gamelike maze. At the beginning of the maze is a blinking light. If your brain is producing a minimum level of brain waves, you can power that blinking light to race through the maze. The blinking stops when your brain moves out of the selected zone of brain wave output and starts again when it gets back into the zone. Depending on which brain waves are being trained up or down, this method can help people learn how to focus their thinking, and can lower tension throughout the body, which in turn results in less pain.

Where can I find a biofeedback practitioner?

The best place to look is the Internet. Check out the Biofeedback Certification of America or the Association for Applied Psychophysiology & Biofeedback at **www.aapb.org**. Both sites have tabs to help you find a practitioner in your area.

Meditation
using the metaphysical to help the physical

Studies show that regular meditation can lower blood pressure, relieve chronic pain, and reduce cortisol levels, a measure of the body's stress. It may also help if you suffer from fibromyalgia, as it can help teach your body how to relax. Dr. Herbert Benson, a Harvard cardiologist, conducted a great deal of research on meditation and found that regular meditation can actually lower autonomic-nervous-system activity—meaning that meditation allows your body to truly relax. Dr. Benson dubbed this phenomenon the relaxation response.

How can something as simple as meditation perform such wonders? There is no hard answer. Most practitioners say it works because it transports both the body and the mind into a uniquely unified state. As meditation teacher Dr. Lawrence Edwards explains, "Meditation is a transformation process. Over time, meditation evolves into a process where you feel a sense of peace and inner freedom. Every time you meditate you are increasing the reservoir of meditative power that you can tap into during stressful or challenging moments."

There are a number of different meditation techniques to consider. Some focus on the breath, requiring you to simply observe yourself breathing in and out; others use a mantra (a sacred word or phrase) that is repeated over and over again. The goal is the same: to focus your attention away from the thoughts whirling around inside your head. The repetition of breath or mantra helps calm the mind so it can enter into a meditative state. Classic meditation does not involve talking or music, but it may be helpful to light a scented candle or burn incense. That's because your mind will associate the fragrance with relaxation, registering that it's time to settle down, and that can help ease your transition. It's also helpful to meditate at the same time every day and for the same amount of time, even if it's only for a few minutes.

How to Meditate

Find a place where you can sit quietly without interruption for 20 minutes.

Sit comfortably, but keep your back erect—this will help support alertness and open breathing. (You can meditate lying down if you are not able to sit up.)

Set a timer for 15 to 20 minutes.

Close your eyes and bring your attention to your breathing. Focus on the movement of your diaphragm as you inhale and exhale.

As you settle into this quiet breathing, you can silently repeat a mantra or any words you wish. You can use the traditional Sanskrit words *Om Namah Shivaya*, silently say a phrase of your own choosing, or simply say the words "one, two, three, four."

When your mind begins to wander, as it inevitably will, just gently return your focus to your breath or mantra. This pattern of wandering and returning is the beginning of teaching your mind to let go of its worries.

When the timer buzzes, notice how peaceful you feel.

Open your eyes and stretch.

Choose a regular time and place to meditate. Start by meditating for 20 minutes three times a week. Stay with it.

Herbs and minerals
nature's medicine chest

There are many herbs and botanicals associated with fibromyalgia relief. If you are considering taking any herbal supplement, you should check with your doctor first. There are a number of drug interactions that can occur. Note, too, that herbs and vitamins are not yet regulated by the FDA. That means it is difficult to know the quantity and quality of the supplement you are taking.

Still, since doctors often prescribe antidepressants for fibromyalgia patients, it's no surprise that what people seek most from the health food stores for their fibromyalgia symptoms are "natural" antidepressants.

Here are the most popular ones:
Magnesium and malic acid.

Found in many foods, especially nuts and whole grains, magnesium is a mineral essential to healthy bone and tissue. Malic acid is found in apples and other fruits. Both of these are involved in the body's production of ATP, a phosphate that provides an energy source in many metabolic processes and is believed to be deficient in people who have fibromyalgia.

Experts believe that when taken together, magnesium and malic acid will offer relief from pain and fatigue, though this has not been proven. Those with kidney problems should avoid taking either. Drawback? Loose stool.

SAM-e.

The term is short for S-adenosylmethionine, an essential molecule naturally occurring in the cells of plants and animals. As we age, our bodies produce less SAM-e, which is believed to help the body produce and regulate hormones and other biochemical substances that affect mood. Some experts think that it may prove helpful in treating depressive symptoms. Others believe it can relieve pain the way NSAIDs do without the stomach-related side effects.

Initial studies show that SAM-e may be effective with depressive symptoms; however, further studies are under way. The drawbacks? It can be expensive and may cause nausea, diarrhea, headache, anxiety, and flatulence. It can also cause a change from bouts of depression to intense periods of energy (mania).

St. John's wort.

One of the most popular herbal supplements, St. John's wort is widely available in supermarkets and health food stores in the U.S. While it has fewer adverse side effects than drugs traditionally prescribed for depression, its effectiveness has not been fully proven. St. John's wort is made from a small yellow wildflower and contains two chemicals, hypericin and hyperforin, which may raise serotonin levels. Serotonin is the brain chemical linked to depression and often found in lower-than-normal levels in those with fibromyalgia. St. John's wort is taken in either pill or liquid form. Drawbacks? Possible increased sensitivity to the sun. Also, St. John's wort should not be used by those who are already taking prescription antidepressants.

Acupuncture
help for chronic pain

There is no published evidence as of yet to support the use of acupuncture for fibromyalgia. But this ancient therapy, which arose in China more than 2,000 years ago, is slowly gaining ground. Acupuncture involves placing fine needles at specific points on the body's surface. According to a 1998 consensus statement from the National Institutes of Health, acupuncture is clearly useful for adults with postoperative and chemotherapy nausea and vomiting, as well as (probably) the nausea of pregnancy. In addition, the National Institutes of Health states that there is promising evidence suggesting the technique can help addiction, stroke rehabilitation, migraine headaches, fibromyalgia, osteoarthritis, lower back pain, carpal tunnel syndrome, asthma, and other problems.

Approximately 9 to 12 million Americans turn to acupuncture each year for relief from chronic medical ailments. But acupuncture isn't a cure-all. It is best used for people with chronic, long-standing pain problems—such as musculoskeletal disorders—as well as for those with nonchronic conditions, such as pain related to injuries and other traumas.

Traditional Chinese practitioners believe acupuncture unblocks and balances the energy or *chi* (sometimes spelled qi) flowing through your body along pathways called meridians. If the flow of chi is blocked or unbalanced at any point in a pathway, illness may result (according to the belief).

Western practitioners who have studied it theorize that acupuncture reduces pain through blocked biological mechanisms possibly involving opioid peptides (the body's own painkillers) and stimulation of the hypothalamus and pituitary gland, or changes in neurotransmitters, hormones, or immune function.

Ask the Experts

How deep are the needles inserted?

Only a few millimeters. The needles are very fine, and discomfort is minimal.

If I use acupuncture do I need anything else?

Practitioners certified in acupuncture may also recommend some herbal treatments.

How do I find a practitioner?

Again, talk to your doctor. Most, but not all, states provide licensing or registration for physician and non-physician acupuncturists. If possible, check to see if your practitioner is certified by the National Certification Commission for Acupuncture and Oriental Medicine. Physicians who use acupuncture in their practices are generally certified by the American Academy of Medical Acupuncture.

Yoga, the "mindful" exercise
using yoga to help you handle your pain

The goals of yogic exercise are to teach you to stay alert to your body as you exercise and to coordinate your breathing with your movements. For these reasons, many people consider yoga a "mindful" exercise, a form of meditation in motion. But how does that help your fibromyalgia? Studies have shown that yoga has a strong antidepressant effect and that it promotes mental and emotional clarity, improves balance, flexibility, strength, and stamina, relieves chronic muscle aches, eliminates stress, and helps to regulate your metabolism. All exercise helps improve circulation, and that in turn can help stave off some of the complications of fibromyalgia. Yoga is especially helpful when used in combination with aerobic exercise, such as brisk walking or bike riding, and traditional strength building, such as working out with light weights.

There are variations in the way yoga is taught. Shop around until you find something that suits you. Some classes are slow-paced; others are as lively as a step-aerobics class. Typically, yoga classes can be paid for one at a time, or in sets of 5 or 10 with a discounted price. Some health clubs offer yoga classes, often at no additional cost to the membership price. If you're curious but skeptical, ask to observe a class; you should be able to do this for free. Class lengths vary; a midday class may be 45 minutes, but an evening class may be 60 or 90 minutes long—and priced accordingly.

Living in the Moment

If you explore meditation and spiritual traditions even a little—and there are many methods and approaches—you will hear a lot about learning to live in the moment. Instead of allowing your thoughts to race ahead to the next task, or to tomorrow, or further in the future, you remain grounded in the here and now, totally and fully present to experience life.

How do you reach that point? Some experts say regular meditation can enable you to achieve that level. Others speak of training yourself to pay attention to the moment. Can it work for you? Try it and see.

Qigong and Tai Chi

According to the National Qigong Association, qigong is "an ancient Chinese health care system that integrates physical postures, breathing techniques, and focused intention." Pronounced "CHEE-gung"—and sometimes spelled Chi Kung—the word means "cultivating energy." Tai chi is a form of qigong; both are practiced for health maintenance, healing, and increased vitality. Tai chi is also a martial art, and the sequence of gestures used there help to prepare the person, mentally and physically, for fighting. Both qigong and tai chi consist of a series of dancelike gestures that are performed in a specific sequence. The sequence of gestures is called a form, and there are long and short forms of the exercises. In tai chi, the short form takes about 10 minutes to complete; it's a bit longer for qigong. Practitioners of the form say that the sense of vitality you feel afterward will last throughout the day.

Chiropractic therapy
it's all in the spine

Chiropractic health care focuses on spinal function and how the spine relates to the nervous system and to overall good health. Despite the fact that some 30 million people seek chiropractic care every year, it still remains a controversial practice in the eyes of some physicians due to chiropractic's nondrug, nonsurgical approach. However, today some physicians are working more closely with doctors of chiropractic, especially when treating back pain.

Chiropractors believe that many ailments are caused by the vertebrae impinging on the spinal nerves. That is, if the spinal or musculoskeletal system is out of alignment, the body cannot function properly. They refer to such interferences with normal nerve transmissions as "subluxations." After a chiropractic "adjustment" to achieve the proper vertebral alignment, they believe, normal brain and nerve transmission are restored and the body is able to regain its ability to recover from illness.

There is a wealth of evidence that chiropractic adjustments have a significant value in treating back pain. By adjusting the spine and other bones of the body, chiropractors can realign the body to a more natural healthy stance. This can ward off unnecessary muscle strain caused from misaligned bones. Most chiropractors use their hands to make these adjustments. While it is hoped that these subtle adjustments will keep your bones in proper alignment over the long-term, they rarely do, and repeat visits are often required. The question is whether chiropractic treatments can help with fibromyalgia. There is as yet no published data that it offers value to those with fibromyalgia.

ASK THE EXPERTS

What kind of training do chiropractors receive?

According to the American Chiropractic Association, doctors of chiropractic must complete four to five years at an accredited chiropractic college and pass the national board exam and all exams required by the state in which they practice. They must also meet all individual state licensing requirements in order to become doctors of chiropractic.

How do I find a chiropractor?

Finding a chiropractor may be as simple as asking your medical doctor for a referral. Otherwise, the American Chiropractic Association has a doctor finder on its Web site at **www.acatoday.org.**

I think my health insurance covers visits to a chiropractor. How do I know for sure?

Very simply, call your health insurer and find out what it covers. Some insurers do cover chiropractic visits but cap the number of visits.

What happens during a chiropractic adjustment? Does it hurt?

After your initial examination, and possibly a series of X-rays, and a health history, the chiropractor will likely "adjust" you by applying hand pressure to areas in and around your vertebrae, which can result in a series of popping or crunching sounds. Some patients report a slight discomfort; others say they feel a sensation of relief after an adjustment, which takes only a few minutes.

Whether or not you will experience relief from your fibromyalgia symptoms is a very individual matter. It's important for you to fully inform the chiropractor about your fibromyalgia—how much you hurt and where specifically. This way, the chiropractor will be more sensitive to your tender areas and offer a more gentle approach. You should also ask how many treatments the chiropractor thinks you will need and what relief you can expect.

Massage and bodywork
the lowdown on getting a rubdown

Bodywork is the catchall word for a range of physical therapies that involve manipulation of the body. It is very helpful at relieving muscle tension brought on by stress and strain. Some people with fibromyalgia also say that a massage helps keep their muscles supple, but there is no documented evidence to support that claim.

People who practice therapeutic massage generally avoid the words "masseuse" and "masseur" and instead call themselves massage therapists. Their ads will state that they practice therapeutic, medical, or sports massage, and in states where the practice is regulated by the government, the abbreviation LMT (licensed massage therapist) may follow the person's name. Another string of letters to look for is NCTMB. This means that the therapist has received at least 500 hours of training and has passed a qualifying exam administered by the National Certification Board for Therapeutic Massage and Bodywork. In states where massage is a licensed health practice, your insurance company may reimburse some of the costs.

When Pain is No Gain

Once you've found a reputable massage therapist (see page 156), preferably one who has dealt with fibromyalgia patients before, you will want to point out areas that are especially painful to you. Ask for the most gentle type of massage. And if it starts to hurt too much, speak up and tell the therapist. A too-vigorous massage can potentially create more pain! If the area is swollen or painful, avoid massage; this may worsen it. Like exercise, massage can be dehydrating, so be sure to drink plenty of water after a massage.

The different practices vary in intensity and therapeutic benefits. In general, massage means Swedish massage and/or shiatsu, and bodywork encompasses a wide range of other physically based therapies. Here's a look at some popular bodywork therapies. (To get more information or for help in locating a practitioner, see page 156).

Swedish massage. Originally intended to help improve blood circulation and encourage drainage of the lymph system, this technique uses gliding, kneading, tapping, or vibrating strokes for gentle or penetrating muscle massage. It is especially helpful for tension relief and relaxation.

Myofascial therapy. This is a general term for a number of techniques that manipulate soft tissue—muscle fibers (*myo-*) and fascia, the connective tissue that holds muscle fibers in place—to relieve trigger points, localized areas that are painful themselves or provoke pain in other areas.

Rolfing. Developed by Ida P. Rolf, a biochemist who called the process Structural Integration, it is a form of deep manipulation of the body's soft tissues to balance energy and relieve chronic pain and stress. Practitioners are trained and certified by the Rolf Institute in Colorado.

Shiatsu (acupressure). This is a component of traditional Chinese medicine. Practitioners use fingertip pressure on specific points along the body's energy channels to release blocks, restore balance, and encourage health.

CranioSacral therapy (CST). This therapy was developed by an osteopath, Dr. John E. Upledger. Practitioners gently manipulate the skull, the sacrum, and the nerve endings in the scalp. It is helpful for back and neck pain, headache, sinus infections, stress and tension, chronic fatigue, and fibromyalgia. Practitioners are trained and certified by the Upledger Institute in Florida.

The Trager Approach. Nonintrusive massage and movement re-education, focusing on integrating the mind and body to relieve anxiety. Practitioners are trained and certified by the Trager Institute in Ohio.

Helpful resources

Alternative Treatments for Fibromyalgia and Chronic Fatigue Syndrome
by Mari Skelly and Andrea Helm

Beyond the Relaxation Response
by Herbert Benson, M.D.

Fibromyalgia and the MindBodySpirit Connection
by William B. Salt II, M.D.

Full Catastrophe Living
by Jon Kabat-Zinn

The Power of Now: A Guide to Spiritual Enlightenment
by Eckhart Tolle

National Center for Complementary and Alternative Medicine (NCCAM)
National Institutes of Health
Bethesda, MD 20892
This government agency provides information about and sponsors research in complementary therapies.
888-644-7227
www.nccam.nih.gov

American Council on Science and Health
1995 Broadway, Second floor
New York, NY 10023-5860
212-362-7044
(Fax) 212-362-4919

Complementary and Alternative Healing University
This site is full of advice and explanations about every kind of alternative treatment under the sun.
www.alternativehealing.org

American College for the Advancement of Medicine
This organization is an excellent resource for finding alternative, licensed doctors practicing in your area.
714-583-7666

Cutting-edge Research

Solving the mystery
researching the cause

Before medical researchers can find a cure for fibromyalgia, they need to find the cause. But because fibromyalgia affects so many aspects of the body, from the brain to the muscles and everything in between, research is spread out in a number of different areas, with many disciplines involved.

The National Institute of Arthritis and Musculoskeletal and Skin Disease (NIAMS) is involved in a broad range of clinical studies. For example, studies are looking into the connection between the hormone cortisol and fibromyalgia. Researchers are examining the regulation of the function of the adrenal glands (which make cortisol) in fibromyalgia. People whose bodies make inadequate amounts of cortisol experience many of the same symptoms as those with fibromyalgia. Scientists are hoping that these studies will shed new light on the disorder and suggest new ways to treat it.

Other NIAMS researchers are investigating the links between sleep and fibromyalgia. One project using mice is looking to identify the factors involved in sleep regulation. This project will screen for single-gene mutations that affect sleep patterns in mice. Scientists are hoping that understanding this process in mice will advance our understanding of human sleep patterns.

Other NAIMS-supported clinical research on fibromyalgia includes:
- Comparing pain mechanisms in the disorder and lower back pain.

- Determining if aerobic exercise benefits those with fibromyalgia through the action of the hypothalamus and pituitary and adrenal glands.

- Studying neuroendocrine changes in fibromyalgia and irritable bowel syndrome.

◆ Examining the effectiveness of combining two antidepressants to treat the disorder.

◆ Investigating the causes of a post-Lyme-disease syndrome as a model for fibromyalgia. Some patients develop a condition similar to fibromyalgia after contracting Lyme disease.

◆ Studying the role of behavioral factors in fibromyalgia for pain management and physical exercise training. The study is designed to test the hypothesis that combining cognitive-behavioral therapy (see pages 58–59) and physical training will be more effective than either alone.

Still other studies are aimed at determining how helpful social support and education are in an individual's handling of fibromyalgia. For instance, a study at Arizona State University is comparing how women with fibromyalgia and women with osteoarthritis cope with pain and stress. The researchers hope to determine which factors lead to improvement and/or worsening of symptoms.

In a 2000 study, the Mayo Clinic in Rochester, Minnesota, found that a three-day interdisciplinary treatment program of evaluation, self-management education about fibromyalgia, and physical and occupational therapy helped reduce symptoms.

New pain-relief drugs
better symptom relief

While the pursuit of the cause of and cure for fibromyalgia continues, researchers are also pursuing new means to help with the symptoms of this disorder. At the moment research seems to point to the fact that fibromyalgia involves some kind of abnormality of the nervous system which results in heightened pain perception. Research has shown that the intensity of pain which people with fibromyalgia report feeling just may correlate with abnormalities in their brains. Several studies show that people with fibromyalgia have less than the normal level of the neurotransmitter serotonin and more of the neuropeptide substance P, both of which are involved in relaying pain messages from nerve cells to the spinal cord and the brain. Drug company researchers are testing a new drug that works in part by reducing Substance P, a pain-transmitting chemical that fibromyalgia sufferers produce in excess.

Meanwhile, drugs that have been approved to help ease the symptoms of such health disorders as Parkinson's and multiple sclerosis are being tried on those with fibromyalgia. For example, one drug, pramipexole, sold under the brand name Mirapex is used to treat the symptoms of Parkinson's. Another drug, tizanidine, sold under the brand name Zanaflex is used to treat the symptoms of muscle spasticity in those with multiple sclerosis and spinal cord injury. Both are being studied as possible treatments for fibromyalgia. In another approach, researchers at McGill University in Montreal are working on the concept of personalized pain prescriptions. Here the type and dosage of drug you get would be based on your genetic markers for hair color, skin tone, and gender. In experiments, researchers have demonstrated that redheaded, fair-skinned mice experienced better pain relief from pentazocine (Talwin), a well-known pain reliever, than white- or dark-skin mice. The results of the study may someday allow doctors to base pain prescriptions on their patients' inherited traits.

What about Guaifenesin?

While it has never been clinically proven to treat fibromyalgia symptoms, some have found relief with **guaifenesin**, an expectorant, found in many common cough syrups. Expectorants work by thinning out and loosening mucus in the respiratory tract, making it easier to cough up.) According to proponents of guaifenesin, dosages must be closely monitored and any exposure to salicylates (a common additive found in cosmetics and toiletries) must be avoided. Taking an over-the-counter cough medicine is not advised. Note: Guaifenesin is not FDA-approved for treating fibromyalgia.

And now for some good news

Even if you never get back to your pre-fibromyalgia self, your condition probably won't get any worse. And if you maintain a healthy lifestyle, it may even improve. This news comes from a Norwegian study of women with fibromyalgia who participated in an exercise and education program in the early 1990s. At intervals of six and eight years after they completed the program, researchers evaluated them on a variety of measures, including body mass index, employment status, and ability to cope with everyday life, as well as their fibromyalgia symptoms.

The results: While all 33 women still reported widespread pain, not all of them—70 percent—still had enough tender points to be considered to have fibromyalgia. And, compared to their conditions six or eight years earlier, the women participating in an exercise program had fewer tender points.

Those who participated in a patient exercise program reported significantly less pain and fatigue. Twenty-six of the women continued to exercise regularly, and those who worked at jobs outside of their homes when the study began continued to do so. While the study's conclusions are far from ideal—the disorder never went completely away—researchers say it is still very hopeful. Over time, the fibromyalgia is likely to get better, even if it never vanishes completely.

Surgery
if you have Chiari malformation

In a 1999 issue of the journal *Neurology,* there was a study showing that people with **Chiari malformation** (an abnormal positioning of the brain stem) had some of the classic symptoms of fibromyalgia and chronic fatigue syndrome. The common symptoms of Chiari malformation are neck pain, headache, weakness in the arms, poor muscle coordination, and abnormal sensations such as tingling or burning. This malformation, which can be seen in an X-ray or MRI (and is usually diagnosed in childhood), can be corrected by surgery.

The surgery to correct this malformation involves removing a small piece of the skull so that the brain stem is no longer squeezed into the funnel of the spinal cord. The surgery usually ends the problematic symptoms of Chiari. What is interesting is that after surgery, people who had severe Chiari malformation as well as symptoms of fibromyalgia and/or CFS reported an end to their CFS and/or fibromyalgia symptoms as well. Did the surgery cure their fibromyalgia? Or was their fibromyalgia actually a manifestation of their Chiari malformation? As yet, no one knows for sure. What is known is that the number of people that might benefit from this surgery is extremely small.

ASK THE EXPERTS

How common is Chiari malformation?

Chiari malformation is rare. This means that the subset of people with both Chiari and fibromyalgia is rarer still.

Is surgery always recommended for Chiari malformation?

Not necessarily. There are several different types of of malformations. Some are quite mild and require no intervention. Others are severe and have resulted in painful symptoms. In those cases, surgery is recommended.

In our fast-paced, competitive culture, isn't just about everyone stressed? How can I tell if I am suffering from stress?

You can begin by paying attention to your body and listening for these key warning signals: tight shoulders, neck or arm muscles; hunched shoulders or clenched teeth. Butterflies or knots in the stomach, loss of appetite, diarrhea or constipation. Anxiety, moodiness, hopelessness, anger, low self-esteem, depression or inability to concentrate. Difficulty falling asleep, waking up early and not being able to fall back to sleep, oversleeping or having disturbing dreams. Chronic tiredness, cold, clammy hands, pounding heart, tightness or heaviness in the chest or a dry mouth.

Clinical trials
how do they work

There are quite a number of current medical studies regarding fibromyalgia. Some studies look to test the effectiveness of a new drug; others are delving into the causes of the syndrome. What these studies all have in common is that they can make use of clinical trials to further their research.

What exactly is a clinical trial? It is a research study using human volunteers to answer very specific health questions. Most clinical trials test a new drug or treatment. A **blind study** is when volunteers do not know if they are receiving the real drug or a **placebo** (a sugar pill). In a **double-blind study**, those administering the medicines or treatment also don't know whether a volunteer is getting the real drug or the placebo, or treatment or nontreatment. This is done to avoid any potential bias on the part of the practitioners. (Only independent monitors have that knowledge.)

When it comes to clinical trials to test new drugs, there are three test phases the drug must pass before the FDA will approve it. In a Phase I test, a small group of human volunteers tests the safety of the drug and identify any side effects. If all goes well, a drug will move into Phase II. Here, more human volunteers are sought to further test the drug for efficacy and dosage strengths. The final Phase III stage requires thousands of people to test the new drug. This is usually when a drug is compared to other drugs on the market as well as to a placebo.

Every clinical trial in the U.S. must be approved and monitored by an Institutional Review Board (IRB) to make sure the risks are as low as possible and are worth any potential benefits. An IRB can stop a study if it appears to be causing unexpected hardship to participants or if there is evidence that the risks outweigh the benefits. Similarly, if there is clear evidence that the new treatment is effective, an IRB can stop a study to make the treatment more widely available.

What questions should I ask before I decide to participate in a clinical trial?

You should prepare the for initial visit as you would for a visit to any doctor (see page 114). Write down a list of questions ahead of time, such as:

◆ What is the purpose of the study, and who will be in it?

◆ What kinds of tests and treatments are involved?

◆ What are the possible risks, side effects, and benefits? Will the study cover the cost of medical care incurred by any adverse effects?

◆ How long will the trial last, and will I need to be hospitalized?

◆ Will I be reimbursed for any expenses or time off work?

◆ Will I be able to find out the results of the trial?

◆ Will any follow-up care be available to me?

FIRST PERSON INSIGHTS

Doing my part

I've never served in the military, or even got called for jury duty, so when I signed up for a clinical trial, I figured it was a kind of civic duty, something I was doing for the greater good. I have to admit, I was a little worried about taking a new drug for fibromyalgia, but they showed me literature that said the new drug had passed all the animal safety tests and a small trial with human subjects.

I am pretty sure I got the real drug and not the placebo, because it did help me to sleep better—and that's exactly what the researchers were trying to determine. I had to stay on the university's campus for a week, and then answer a lot of questions about how I felt and how well I slept. I met other people in trial and we talked a lot about our fibro. I even exchanged e-mail addresses with some. Best of all were the doctors and scientists running the trials. They were totally professional, yet very caring. I learned a lot from them about how best to handle my fibromyalgia.

—Margot V., Seattle, WA

Helpful resources

For information on
medical research:
www.centerwatch.com

**The Fibromyalgia Research
Center**
University of Washington
Medical Center
1959 N.E. Pacific Street
Box 356540
Seattle, WA 98195
206-221-5146
fibroct@u.washington.edu

**The American Fibromyalgia
Syndrome Association, Inc.**
6380 E. Tanque Verde
Suite D
Tucson, AZ 85715
520-733-1570
www.afsafund.org

**The National Fibromyalgia
Association**
2200 Glassell Street
Suite A
Orange, CA 92865
718-921-0150
www.fmaware.org

The National Library of Medicine
A service of the National Institutes
of Health, offers excellent explanations about clinical trials as well as
links to other useful medical sites.
www.nlm.nih.gov/services

CHAPTER 11

Stress and Fibromyalgia

What is stress?
it's not just a built-in survival mechanism

Stress has become the watchword for a number of medical problems today. It seems that stress can cause certain illnesses as well as worsen your symptoms once you become ill. How can something be both a cause and an effect? The answer lies in the complex nature of stress, or rather our complex reaction to it. While scientists have learned a great deal more about the nature of stress in the past few years, they are still baffled by it. One of the most puzzling aspects of stress is that its effect on our bodies is based on how we perceive stressful situations. Some stressors can help us perform at our peak abilities; other stressors can be debilitating. It's all in the eye of the beholder. So far, the one thing researchers agree upon is that the number-one reason for negative stress is the perception of not being in control. Not having control over one's life or environment can be a very threatening feeling and can easily trigger the stress response, be it for a short duration or the long term.

A perceived short-term threat

This stressor could be a lunging tiger, an oncoming car, an angry boss, or a physical symptom. Reacting to threats is so critical to our survival that our bodies are designed to either fight or flee the threat. Here's how our bodies handle it: When a threat is perceived, the brain's hypothalamus sends out an alarm to the sympathetic nervous system to release adrenaline into the blood stream. This increases your heart rate and blood pressure so you can run or fight. While this response is intended to heighten our reaction to potentially dangerous situations, it does not necessarily prepare us for rational thought or decision-making. Note: The perceived threat is always in the eye of the beholder. The stress response will occur whether the threat is real or imagined. (This is why your heart races during a scary movie.)

The brain also signals the adrenal glands to release two key stress hormones called **epinephrine** and **norepinephrine**. These hormones increase the glucose levels in the blood so that muscles can effectively respond. This is why some people can perform incredible feats of strength in a crisis.

Once the threat has passed, the brain issues an all-clear signal. Special cells in the brain send out signals to the major organs to return to normal. This allows the digestive system to go back to the business of digesting food, and the heart rate and blood pressure to return to a calmer beat. Essentially, the body is told to relax—the threat has passed. If the threat lasted for a few minutes, ideally it would take just a few minutes to return to normal. But what if it is considered a chronic threat? That is another story.

Women and Stress

Women react differently than men. For the past 50 years, stress research was done on male animals. It was from their response to various stressors that researchers came up with the catchphrase, "fight or flight." That changed in 1998 when researcher Shelley E. Taylor thought to study the stress response in female animals. Dr. Taylor found that females responded differently to non-life-threatening stress, particularly if they were tending young offspring. The female animals did not become nearly as alarmed as their male counterparts. In fact, their reaction was to tend to their young and to seek comfort in other females. Dr. Taylor went on to test her theory on men and women and found that in general men tend to isolate themselves when they feel stressed, while women confide their problems to each other. As Dr. Taylor describes it in her book, *The Tending Instinct*, women "tend and befriend."

Chronic stress
be alert to coping patterns

What happens when a perceived threat lingers for days or weeks? Long-term negative stressors, such as going through a messy divorce, becoming ill, or getting laid off from work, can all go on for months, even years. This means the all-clear signal is never given by the brain, so the body never gets a chance to return to equilibrium. It's as if the body is on a constant state of alert. Over time, this can take a physical toll on the body, especially if these stressors are perceived to be negative threats. A kind of learned helplessness can set in, a feeling that events are out of one's control, which can lead to lowered motivation, and self-esteem, and to a sense of helplessness. Again, perception is key. This is why some people thrive on such stressors as deadlines for a long-term project they are passionate about, while others who don't feel emotionally involved or in control of their work feel stressed out.

When it comes to long-term stress, having a sense of control is crucial. Long-term negative stress can lead to bouts of anxiety, aggression, and depression. Some scientists believe that chronic stress has a harmful effect on the immune system and the endocrine system, making people more vulnerable to illness and infection. Whether you have an illness or not, when it comes to chronic stress you need to work on improving your coping skills.

So, how do you cope with long-term stress? For starters, look at how you have coped in the past with other chronic stressors, especially negative ones. Did you isolate yourself from friends and family? Did you seek out comfort foods? Sleep a lot? Fall into bad habits, such as overeating or drinking? Try to see if there is a pattern to how you coped. It's also a good idea to recall how your parents or other significant caregivers handled negative stressors. You may have internalized their coping responses and not realized it.

Negative coping responses

There are several negative coping responses that we all have used at one time or another when dealing with long-term stress. Here is a roundup:

- **Deny your problems**. This is a common response for many people—they simply ignore their problems. Often, to help take their minds off their problems, they throw themselves into their work or social life.

- **Dwell on your problems**. Again, this is usually a learned response. Did your parents or caregivers fret excessively over your health as you were growing up? Or did they ignore your health completely? If they sought either of these extremes, you may find yourself obsessing about your health. If these thoughts become chronic, you should see a therapist who can help you break the pattern of obsessive rumination.

- **Procrastinate in decision-making**. Instead of thinking through the problems at hand, you endlessly analyze the situations, and talk about the same problems and solutions over and over again with friends and family.

- **Seek thrills**. Here you look for thrills or experiences to distract you from your problems.

- **Get angry and lash out at others**. This is known as displaced aggression. It's when you take out your anger at being ill on others and overreact to their responses.

- **Withdraw**. This can take the form of physically or emotionally withdrawing from others. Often people under chronic stress will cope by sleeping excessively or simply by disengaging from the world.

- **Overindulge**. Food is used as a drug to mask fears as well as boredom. Too much alcohol is another way to cope with all the problems of chronic stress, and so is smoking too many cigarettes or cigars.

Assault on mind and body
stress can lead to other physical ailments

The event that triggers stress can be good (a promotion) or bad (a diagnosis of a chronic illness). Hundreds of studies show that stress aggravates illness—chronic or episodic, life-threatening or curable. Uncontrolled stress can weaken the immune system and make a person more prone to other health problems, such as colds, flu, general malaise, and fatigue.

◆ Chronic stress can exacerbate or even trigger hair loss, make wounds heal more slowly, and cause a person to become prone to such dermatological problems as adult acne, rashes, eczema, and hives.

◆ High stress can lead to binge eating, resulting in obesity, which can lead to a host of problems, such as heart disease and diabetes.

◆ High stress levels—along with negative emotions—release high levels of cortisol. Blood-pressure and cholesterol levels go up.

◆ Reproduction can be difficult since chronic stress compromises the reproductive hormones for both men and women.

◆ Severe gastrointestinal problems are also common, from exacerbation of the symptoms of ulcers to aggravation of already sensitive bowels.

◆ Chronic muscle tension due to chronic stress can make arthritis flare-ups worse and exacerbate lower back problems.

◆ The chronically stressed can have mild memory loss and problems with concentrating or organizing thoughts.

◆ If you have any bad habits, they will get worse with chronic stress. Smoking, binge drinking, and drug abuse have all been linked to chronic stress.

You swear you're going to melt down he next time someone asks you exactly what fibromyalgia is. As an alternative, though, here's a handy, abbreviated explanation, as well as answers to the inevitable questions friends and coworkers will ask:

◆ Fibromyalgia is a chronic pain condition characterized by widespread pain, muscular stiffness especially in the morning, fatigue, disturbed sleep, and overall distress.

◆ Unfortunately, there is no cure at the moment, but scientists are working on it.

◆ Fibromyalgia can be managed by treating the symptoms with pain reducers, sleep medications, exercise, and complementary methods such as massage therapy and biofeedback.

◆ No, it is not contagious, and yes, women are more apt to be afflicted than men are.

◆ Yes, it is sometimes brought on by a trauma, such as a car accident or an illness, which causes the body's pain-processing system to go awry.

◆ The symptoms of fibromyalgia wax and wane. Those who have it experience good days and also flares, in which the symptoms "flare-up" or intensify.

◆ Touch that is not painful to a normal individual can cause a person with fibromyalgia to hit the ceiling.

◆ Yes, it is possible to live well with it, with some adjustments.

Smart coping strategies
find positive ways to cope with chronic problems

Having a chronic illness like fibromyalgia in which the symptoms can be dormant for days and then suddenly flare up, can tap your coping reserves. Your old favorite coping standbys may work, but not for long. The challenge of coping with a long-term illness is understanding how to live with it. This calls for a new way of looking at your health and at illness. Since there is no cure yet for many chronic illnesses, the goal becomes the reduction of discomfort and the improvement in your emotional and physical well-being. That means really listening to your symptoms and addressing them. Your goal is simply to improve your quality of life. Here are some coping tips to help you on your way:

Create a fibromyalgia retreat. We all need a place of our own to retreat to when the going gets tough. This is especially vital when you feel fatigued or uncomfortable from the pain of fibromyalgia. For most of us, this retreat is our bedroom. For tips on how to stock your bedroom with helpful supplies, see pages 194–195.

Get organized. Time management becomes a tool you can use when you have fibromyalgia. Your time and energy are now precious commodities that should not be wasted. Learn how to separate those things you really need to do from those you can spread out over time or delegate to others.

Develop healthy habits. Ironically, people often become healthier once health problems have been diagnosed. This may be because they suddenly stop taking their health for granted and turn negative habits into healthy ones, such as eating healthily, or quitting smoking.

Make attitude adjustments. Life with any chronic problem can make the world a dour place. Put some humor back in your life. Rent funny movies, or read humorous books and magazines.

I have to travel for work. How can I cut down on stress while I am on the road?

Traveling is a big stressor, and doubly so if you have to manage a chronic illness while you are on the road. It's smart to be proactive and plan ahead as much as possible. For starters, create a mini-health file with the phone numbers and contact information for all of the people on your support team (see Chapter 7). Make sure to bring extra medication just in case. Next, don't just pack for your trip. Bring a bit of home with you. Include a pair of comfortable jeans or a favorite shawl. Some people who hate to travel bring photos of their family and put them in their hotel room. Don't forget to bring a novel, computer games, knitting, or whatever you like to do to relax. Your goal is to detoxify the stress of travel with things that instantly signal comfort and relaxation.

FIRST PERSON INSIGHTS

Living with fibromyalgia

"I spent about five years being stressed about having fibromyalgia. My kids felt bad, my husband felt bad, my friends felt bad, and so did I. I was constantly worried about my poor health, so much so that I would cancel outings if I felt even a twinge of pain. Looking back, I lost a lot of time being stressed out—which is kind of funny since I'm a registered nurse and I should know better. The only solution I found was to find a doctor who actually talked to me about my fibromyalgia and my worry—in combination. She referred me to a support group. A lot of the people in the group became my friends. I don't have a magic cure for stress. All I do know is that talking to other people really helped me. Plus, I do go on the Internet and leave messages on fibromyalgia boards, especially when I hear about a new treatment or something. I like to listen to other people's opinions, and it's nice to know you're not alone. "

—Marcy N., Nyack, TN

Take a stress inventory
how fibromyalgia can stress you

No one wants to think that his or her stress levels are out of control, but sometimes it is necessary to confront the stress of a health problem head-on. One way is to take a personal stress inventory by asking some tough questions, especially if you feel your fibromyalgia is overwhelming your life—despite treatment. Consider the following questions as they may apply to you:

- ◆ Are you having difficulty accepting a diagnosis of fibromyalgia and the fact that there is no cure?

- ◆ Are you getting disgusted with trying new medications, none of which seem to work for you?

- ◆ Are you spending a lot of time—to the exclusion of all else—researching fibromyalgia and other illnesses?

- ◆ If your fibromyalgia is not responding to treatment, do you hesitate to plan social outings with friends or family because you're afraid of another flare?

These questions aren't scientific. But they do provide a starting point to assess how the stressors of living with fibromyalgia may be affecting you. Again, it doesn't really matter if your symptoms occur once a month, three times a week, or an hour here and there filled with pain. The point is that you have an extra stress in your life—fibromyalgia. If any of these questions seem particularly pertinent to you, talk to your health professional. He or she may be able to allay some of your fears. A support group (see pages 118–119) can also be helpful in allowing you to share your experiences with others who have fibromyalgia. And if no one close to you understands the disease, educate them (see page 188). Stress is part of life. Do not let the stress of the fibromyalgia take control of your life.

Find Good Listeners

Don't be surprised if, when you mention that you have fibromyalgia your listener immediately cuts you off and tells you about his friend's experience with it. Why does that happen, you wonder. Your friend may be trying to gain a sense of involvement in your plight and show that he has some experience with or knowledge of your situation, that he is capable of understanding your pain. But sometimes it can also be a way to create distance. By telling another person's story, he takes you out of the spotlight and puts his friend in it. This can give him a needed sense of control and distance while he absorbs your news.

Ideally, you want your friends to be good listeners—maybe ask a few questions but still keep the focus on you. Since it can be uncomfortable to hear about a total stranger's problems when you have just revealed your own, tell your friend you are not ready to talk about your illness in detail. Then change the subject. Be sure to tell your friend that you would appreciate that he not share your news with others, if that is what you wish.

Learning to relax
beat chronic stress at its own game

Our bodies are brilliantly designed to handle stress. They are also designed to handle relaxation. In fact, both the stress response and the relaxation response are hardwired into our brains. Doctors are just now beginning to understand the power of relaxation upon the body—both to rejuvenate and to heal.

Think back to a time when you felt truly relaxed. What was going on? You were probably in a quiet, comfortable space where you had no pressures to do anything and could sit back and enjoy the day. You felt peaceful and at one with the world. For most people that is the definition of a vacation. Here's the news flash: To be healthy, your body needs a little vacation every day. How do you achieve that? Here are some tips:

Quiet time. Carve out 10 minutes of the day to simply sit and be quiet. Meditation practices are very helpful in teaching people how to quiet their minds and relax. See pages 140–141 for more on this.

Deep breathing. When we are stressed, our breathing becomes shortened, so much so that we can hyperventilate when faced with acute stress. Counter this natural instinct by purposefully taking four deep breaths every time you feel stressed. Breathe in through your nose, hold the breath for five seconds, and then release the air through your mouth.

Exercise. Chronic muscle tension is part and parcel of a chronic stress response. Counteract it by taking a walk or playing a round of tennis. Your goal is to keep your body limber and to keep it moving. For a more relaxing exercise, consider taking a class in yoga or tai chi (see pages 156–157 for more information). Note: Massage is a great way to help rid your muscles of stress-related tension (see pages 160–161).

I have been anxious for so long, I don't think anything will help. What can I do?

If you have been enduring chronic stressors for a long period of time, trying to relax overnight is not going to work. In fact, it will just make you more stressed. You need to retrain your body to feel and behave relaxed. Consider taking a short-term workshop to help you learn how to relax. Your doctor can refer you to a stress clinic or a stress specialist. You can take courses on stress management. The American Management Association offers two-day workshops on managing stress; call them at 800-262-9699. Or try your local YMCA or YMHA; both usually offer stress management classes.

I hear writing about stressful events helps you get over them. True?

Some studies show that writing about stressful issues or traumatic experiences can help improve the immune system. Use your health journal (see pages 16–17) to write about your concerns.

Getting People to Understand

It can be hard to try to explain what it's like to have a chronic health problem to those who have never had one, especially one like fibromyalgia where you don't look sick. Try to find an analogy that works. Most working people can relate to the experience of being laid off. Having a chronic illness is a lot like getting laid off. In both cases, it happens through no fault of your own. And there is a sense of being an outsider—you miss your work routine and feel cut off from the "normal" working world. You also are concerned about your future and are anxious to get back to your old life.

Your partner's concerns
how chronic illness can impact relationships

When one half of a couple has a chronic illness, both members usually need to reassess their partnership. If it's a temporary illness, then it's usually a question of juggling practical matters, such as who will pick up the kids while you're sick in bed. But when symptoms are no longer signs of a temporary illness, but the manifestation of a lingering health problem, a bigger reassessment is needed.

When it comes to handling the ordeals of fibromyalgia, couples need to look at each partner's role and responsibilities in the relationship. You have to state what changes need to be made. This may mean reassigning roles, be it cleaning duties or paying the bills, when a fibromyalgia flare strikes. Often couples fall into the trap in which one becomes the dominant caregiver and the other becomes the professional patient. Try to avoid that dynamic, because it usually leads to resentment on both sides. It's a good idea to have your partner come along with you on a doctor's visit so that he or she sees firsthand what it is like to be a patient.

Money may become an issue if you do not have adequate health insurance or need to cut back on work. Sometimes fibromyalgia can affect your love life, because you may feel too exhausted to have sex. Talk about your concerns and listen to your partner. The important thing is to keep the lines of communication open and not to shut down. A good therapist, knowledgeable about the effects of chronic disease on sexuality, may be able to help you work through these issues. To find a therapist for your particular concern, start at the American Association of Sex Educators, Counselors, and Therapists (**www.aasect.org**).

Since the fibromyalgia started two years ago, I am not the person I used to be. I really worry about my marriage because my husband ends up doing a lot around the house. I'm scared to death he will get so sick of it all, he will leave me.

"Your prior history is important. It's not as if you woke up one day and had fibromyalgia and the 10 years before that were irrelevant," says Dennis Turk, a clinical psychologist at the University of Washington's medical school and the director of its Fibromyalgia Research Center. "The quality of your family relationship beforehand is important in how the family responds. If you've had a good marriage, it's likely your family will respond differently than if you have struggled in the past and had a troubled relationship."

If you feel overwhelmed, or concerned about how much the situation is taking a toll on your marriage, you might speak to a trained professional.

Making an appointment with a specialist, either a marriage or family therapist or a licensed social worker, can be very helpful in teaching you ways to communicate your needs, fears, and expectations in a more productive way. For help in locating a specialist in your area, see pages 120.

Talking about it
learn how to talk about your needs

For a lot of people, talking about their health issues is torturous. They just don't know how to do it. They don't want to come across as whiners, nor do they want to seem overly dramatic. And so they say nothing. If this sounds familiar, then it's time to learn how to talk about having a chronic illness like fibromyalgia. If you have frequent fibromyalgia flare-ups that are very severe, for example, you should tell your friends and family about what you have learned about the disease. Even if you have mild and infrequent fibromyalgia flare-ups, you still have a chronic illness. Here are a few tips to make talking about it easier:

- ◆ Pick the time and place to talk. You need to set a time and place that is comfortable for you. Don't get backed into talking about your illness when you are not ready. You need to feel in control of the conversation; picking the place and time will help you feel in charge.

- ◆ Rehearse out loud in front of a mirror before you actually talk to your spouse or friends. Simply saying the words ahead of time can help you get over your shyness.

- ◆ Set the terms and limits of the information you want to share. You are the one in charge here; don't let anyone take over the conversation and ask you invasive questions. Simply call a halt to the questions and say you don't feel comfortable answering them right now. Also, set the terms of your information. If you don't want this information shared with others, then say so.

Not talking about it
know when to keep quiet

It's only natural to assume that because something interests you intensely, then it must also interest everyone else. And if that something is as all-important as your fibromyalgia, your family and close friends will surely want to know every detail, and even casual acquaintances will be fascinated by the dramatic story line. Wrong. Remind yourself every day that a good conversationalist is first of all a good listener.

Five Rules for Talking about Your Illness

1. "How are you?" is a greeting, not a request for medical news. Just because you have a chronic illness, there is no reason to change your usual response. Wait until someone asks specifically about your illness before telling the person about it.

2. Fit the answer to your audience. Have a short version and a long version ready. Your spouse may want to hear every detail the minute you come from your doctor's visit. But your colleagues want only a summary version.

3. Watch for eyes glazing over. Someone has asked about your illness and seems really interested. So you launch into the long version. Watch for signs of boredom. Do they fidget? Glance around? If you pause or ask a question, is there a slight delay before you have their attention again?

4. After about three minutes, change the subject. Even the most loving friend may not be able to take in every detail of an extended medical report. Give them a break. If someone is really interested, they'll return to the subject.

5. Use humor. Have a couple of jokes handy to break up your monologue, or provide an exit line.

On the job
providing proper medical care is smart business

Lisa M. has fibromyalgia. Today, she woke up exhausted and has terrible pain in her neck and lower back. Even though she's taking a drug that is supposed to help with the pain, it will take all her energy to get up and hopefully take a hot shower. She knows she can't go to work, but she has called in sick twice this month already. The sixth time this year. Lisa is certain her coworkers are angry. Worse yet, she thinks her boss is ready to let her go.

Sound familiar? If you're a person with fibromyalgia, one of the toughest stressors is the job. The problem with having fibromyalgia is that for now researchers have yet to find any underlying organic cause for it. There is no infection or disease process. The pain you feel has no cause, thus it is considered a "self-reported" disease. In other words, you have debilitating pain because you say you do. This can be very hard for bosses to understand. They may feel you are shirking your work or trying for an easy out. The only solution here is to try to inform your boss about the nature of fibromyalgia. Take heart; most bosses will try to accommodate you. If your boss doesn't and demotes or fires you, you can file for discrimination through the Americans with Disabilities Act, or ADA.

If you do need to quit work and go on disability, it is vital that you have a doctor who understands fibromyalgia and can explain your condition to your disability insurance carrier.

I am between jobs and don't have any health insurance right now. How do I find inexpensive health insurance that will cover my fibromyalgia?

You want to consider health insurance coverage that is based on membership instead of employment. Consider joining a trade or professional organization that has its own health insurance. For example, if you are a graphic artist, you can join the AIGA, the American Institute of Graphic Artists. It has an insurance plan for its members, and once you join you can become eligible for coverage.

I have had to miss a couple of days of a workshop due to a fibromyalgia flare-up. Should I tell my boss about my illness?

This is totally up to you. It is not necessary to go public about your health to your employer, unless your performance at work is suffering because of it. Only you can know that. Everyone gets sick from time to time. You should not be made to feel guilty about taking your allotted sick days. If you find you need more time off because of your fibromyalgia, then yes, you do need to explain your situation to your boss. See pages 188–189 on how to talk about having a chronic illness. You need to work with your boss to accommodate both your health needs and the needs of the business.

Helpful resources

The Chronic Illness Workbook
by Patricia A. Fennel

*Who Moved My Cheese? An
Amazing Way to Deal with Change
in Your Work and in Your Life*
by Spencer Johnson, M.D. and
Kenneth H. Blanchard

*Managing Stress: Principles and
Strategies for Health and Well-Being*
(with CD-ROM)
by Brian Luke Seaward

*The Relaxation & Stress
Reduction Workbook*
by Martha Davis et al.

*Instant Relief: Tell Me Where It
Hurts and I'll Tell You What to Do*
by Peggy W. Brill and
Susan Suffes

*Mind, Stress, and Emotions:
The New Science of Mood*
by Gene Wallenstein

**www.psychosocialnetwork.org/
faq_stress.htm**

www.4woman.gov/faq/

www.yourmedicalsource.com/

Dealing with Setbacks

Your symptoms return
what's going on?

You can be taking pain meds and antidepressants, having weekly massages to relax. Then, suddenly, you wake up feeling awful. You are experiencing a fibromyalgia flare, or flare-up. Some (or all) of your symptoms have resurfaced, after having been dormant for some time. This is the nature of many chronic syndromes and what sets them apart from a short-lived acute illness.

As the name suggests, a chronic illness never goes away. The symptoms might disappear, leading you to believe they're gone for good. But then they return, and you feel as if you're back to square one. At that point, you need to examine what's going on in your life. Stress can be a huge contributor to a flare-up. That includes bad as well as good stress. Your body can't tell the difference between the two.

Or it might be something as simple as a medicine that's no longer working as it did. Or maybe you just forgot to take it. Depending upon the severity of your flare-up, the doctor may want you to schedule an appointment to examine you and rule out other things. Then again, after hearing of your circumstances, he may decide that you are in the midst of a flare-up and recommend a course of action.

The Long View

Any number of things can be happening when you experience a flare-up. It's a wise idea to examine all areas of your life, says Dr. Terence Starz, a clinical professor of rheumatology at the University of Pittsburgh and a practicing rheumatologist. "You need to take a look at your diet, your weight, exercise, your emotional situation, your sleep patterns, and make sure you have realistic goals and expectations," he tells his fibromyalgia patients. To underscore this point, Dr. Starz explains to his patients that with some conditions you measure time on your watch, but with others, like fibromyalgia, you tell time on the calendar. "You need to follow this condition over a long period of time," he says. In other words, occasional setbacks are inevitable.

FIRST PERSON INSIGHTS
Learning to manage

I never considered myself a 'depressed' person. Oh sure, my life has had its share of ups and downs, yet I always bounced back and never wallowed in sadness. After my fibromyalgia diagnosis, things changed. Whether it was chemical, or just the sheer burden of trying to manage everything day-to-day—the job, the house, the family—I found myself overwhelmingly sad. Most of the time, I hid this from everyone, even my husband.

But eventually, things caught up with me, and I had no energy for anything. Most of the time, I just wanted to curl up and sleep it all off. I was falling apart and feeling very scared. Eventually, with a lot of prodding from my husband and my sister, I made an appointment to talk to a psychologist. It took a lot to even get to her office, because I was so uncomfortable about it all. But having the chance to talk to a trained person about how angry, disappointed, and sad I was has been very helpful.

I've learned ways to cope, to manage, and it's helped. I'd recommend this route for anyone whose feelings have become unmanageable.

—Sally C., Dallas, TX

Managing the negativity
breaking the cycle of negative thoughts

Dr. Dennis Turk, Ph.D., a clinical psychologist who heads the University of Washington School of Medicine's Fibromyalgia Research Center, has written extensively on the "downward spiral" of depressed thinking. "Negative thoughts have the effect of increasing your anxiety and pain because they focus on catastrophe and resentment, creating a reality where the worst seems bound to happen and you are the helpless victim," he says. "Your body reacts by tensing. As your body tightens, your pain increases and your sleep may be impaired." Once started, the momentum of your negative thoughts will carry you down, "unless you break out of the pattern."

If you can learn how to change the way you think, Dr. Turk says, you can learn to change the ideas that fuel the anxiety, depression, and anger that invariably worsen your symptoms. Here is a rundown of his method for shattering the cycle. The first step is to identify the type of negative thoughts that may be dominating you, for example:

- **Blaming.** Making someone else responsible for your pain.

- **Self-putdowns.** "Should" statements usually imply that you were stupid, foolish, or weak for not living up to some standard, e.g., "I shouldn't react to pain like this."

- **Polarized thinking.** Everything is black or white, with no gray area. If you suffer a flare-up, then you are likely to think that the efforts you have been making don't count. This is not the case.

- **"Catastrophizing".** You imagine the worst possible outcome and then react as if it will come true. "What if" statements characterize this kind of thinking and add to anxiety levels.

- **Control fallacies.** If you assign a doctor or a clinic total power over your fate, you'll make yourself a powerless victim of your pain.

◆ **Emotional reasoning.** This type of thinking assumes that what you feel must therefore be true. If you feel grief at the notion of never jogging again, then you must be right. You will never jog again.

◆ **Filtering.** This is when you see your pain and fatigue through tunnel vision, filtering out any potentially positive aspects.

◆ **Entitlement fallacy.** Some people with fibromyalgia or other chronic illnesses feel as if they are "entitled" to a symptom-free existence, and believe they should not have to suffer pain or fatigue. They feel cheated and dwell on thoughts that life is unfair.

The next step is to restructure your negative thinking and turn it around. Dr. Turk offers this advice: "Consider paying attention to your thoughts and how they relate to your symptoms. Identify the thoughts that are making things worse in terms of your symptoms or flare-ups. Next, look at your behavioral response to those negative thoughts and try to think of an alternative way of interpreting a situation that results in more positive actions and behavior." Here is a simple way to remember it: Use the ABCD list.

A= **Acknowledge the negative thought.** What built up to that thought?

B= **Behavior.** What was your response to that thought?

C= **Consequences.** What were the consequences of your behavior? Response?

D= **Dispute the negative thought.** Try to come up with a more positive way of looking at things.

Colds and flu
they will hit you harder than others

Doctors and other experts agree that people with fibromyalgia have a normal immune system and don't get colds or other infections any more often than other people do. That's the good news. The bad news is that colds and respiratory infections can aggravate your fibromyalgia symptoms, and it may take you longer to recover from them. If you develop bronchitis, for example, the persistent coughing can intensify the pain in your upper back. A fever may decrease your stamina. Viruses can lead to temporary relapses of your fatigue syndromes. The key once again is patience. Pace yourself, and allow your body to take the time it needs to fully recover.

How do you tell if it's a fibromyalgia flare-up or if you are sick with something else, such as the flu, which is also characterized by muscular aches? Some of the symptoms are similar; others are exactly the same.

One way is to keep track of your symptoms on a chart marked off at hourly intervals throughout the course of your waking hours. For example, at 7:00 A.M., upon awakening, you felt stiff and achy; at 8:00 A.M. you were more relaxed, feeling looser.

The Arthritis Foundation's book, *Good Living with Fibromyalgia* offers excellent illustrated examples, complete with charts and spreadsheets for helping you to track symptoms. Not only will this help you to realize when you are suffering from something other than your fibromyalgia, but it will also be useful when you visit your doctor.

ASK THE EXPERTS

I'm sniffling and sneezing. Is it okay for me to take an over-the-counter decongestant or antihistamine, considering that I'm already taking a shelf full of other, prescription medications for my fibromyalgia?

Stop! Before you add any new medicine to your regimen, whether over-the-counter or prescription, check with your doctor. There may be drug interactions that you don't know about. Keep the doctor informed of all the medicines you are taking at any given time. You may also want to check with your pharmacist. Many pharmacies keep your records on a sophisticated database, and some programs enable the pharmacist to determine immediately whether one medicine will interfere with another. Be sure to also read the information packet that comes with your prescription medicines. This will tell you the other drugs that may not work well with the one you're taking. Some combinations are not affected; others can be deadly.

FIRST PERSON INSIGHTS

Telling the difference

The achiness and pain of my fibromyalgia is very different, to me at least, than when I have a cold or flu. The fibromyalgia is a constant nagging ache, which will flare up to a pain so intense that even picking something up sends waves of pain up and down my arm. Stairs can be like climbing a mountain. A flu, on the other hand, brings more a feeling of heaviness, a weakness. I'm not really weak from the fibro, it's just that the pain at times is so intense that I can't manage simple tasks. I do try to fight my way through it, and usually succeed. I'm trying to apply a "mind-over-matter" philosophy. It works occasionally, mostly when I am not tired. When I am tired, I take to my bed when I need to. Sometimes I don't need the sleep, per se, just the rest, so I take a magazine or headphones with me and just let my body rest. It makes a huge difference.

— Tonianne W., Atlanta, GA

When you need to rest
some practical coping tips

When a flare-up happens, taking to your bed often seems to be the only solution. Don't fall into that comforting trap. Your bed is for sleep and sex and is not to be embraced as a lifestyle. What you want to do is learn to give yourself permission to rest and slow your pace. Here are some practical tips to help:

- ◆ Set up your computer, preferably a laptop, so you can surf the Web, send e-mails, and post and read messages on fibromyalgia boards, without straining your neck.

- ◆ Invest in a three-tiered cart on wheels, which can hold your books, paperwork, drinks, and snacks. Put it by your favorite chair.

- ◆ Leave a note on the door for FedEx, UPS, and mail carriers specifying that packages can be left with certain neighbors. This way, you won't be awakened or disturbed by an insistent doorbell when a delivery person stops by with a package.

- ◆ Order postage stamps by mail, or even through the Web, so you have a ready stock on hand. This will make bill-paying easier and eliminate a post-office stop for you.

- ◆ Keep bags of prepared salads on hand. These can easily be doctored up with cubes of cheese, pregrilled strips of chicken breast or chunks of tuna for an instant, satisfying meal.

- ◆ Keep some self-stick notes by your bedside for lists, reminders, and notes to family and friends that you can stick on the outside of your door.

◆ Have a box of baby wipes near your favorite chair to clean your hands and face throughout the day.

◆ Don't stay in the same position for longer than 30 minutes. Be sure to get up and walk around. Also do gentle stretches every hour or so to keep your muscles from stiffening up.

◆ Create a filing system complete with clipboard to help to keep all paperwork organized and in one place.

◆ Always store your health journal and pain diary in the same place so you can find it easily. Use it to track your symptoms and record your feelings.

◆ If you have children, elderly family members, or animals that need your attention, have backup plans in place in case you can't manage their needs.

Rearranging the house
preparing your household for a setback

It's bound to happen. After a spell of feeling as if you could conquer the world, one day you will wake up feeling awful. It's part of the ebb and flow of fibromyalgia and other chronic conditions.

In an ideal world, you would focus primarily on caring for, even pampering, yourself, resting up to regain your strength. But in the real world, your retreat could spell disaster. So many things that you do—child care, looking after elderly parents, grocery shopping, meal preparation, your job—would fall by the wayside.

For this reason, it's best to have an emergency plan in place. Now's the time to set the wheels in motion and figure it out before you experience a flare-up.

To begin with, take a good look at the overall structure of the way your household is run. Perhaps you can reshuffle duties and responsibilities among various family members to keep your household running smoothly. The changes can be as simple as assigning the youngest family member to feed the dog and keep her water dish filled. If it's affordable, perhaps you can hire someone to help with the heavier cleaning. Or perhaps, if none of that is practical, you need to consider major changes, such as moving into a smaller house or apartment, one without steep stairs or other impediments.

Of course, you can't expect everyone to be comfortable with the changes. Experts recommend that you include everyone in the decision-making process, and that you do it gradually. Think of it as a household brainstorming session in which everyone offers suggestions, no matter how crazy the ideas may sound. Later, you refine the list of suggestions and adopt the practical ones.

Some families swear by lists or charts on a white board to keep track of everyone's duties. Otherwise, it's easy for family members to forget or to argue over whose turn it is to haul out the recyclables. What works for one family isn't necessarily effective for another. Experiment until you determine what's best for yours.

Explaining Flare-ups to Friends and Family

You were okay the other day, so how can you really be that sick now? This morning, merely showering and dressing has left you debilitated, and you're spending the day at rest. You detect skepticism, even downright disbelief, when you tell everyone why you've cancelled all activities for the day.

Most people simply don't understand the nature of chronic pain. Just as you are grappling with the disappointment of all you've had to give up because of your fibromyalgia, your friends and family members are dealing with similar feelings, grieving over the loss of the old you. So they act out and treat you with skepticism, or even hostility.

While fibromyalgia has been around for centuries, it was only identified and named as recently as 1990, when it was formally categorized by the American College of Rheumatology. So if it's still relatively new to the medical community, you can't expect people to fully understand and accept it yet.

Quit the blame game
it's not your fault

If you didn't get enough calcium in your youth and you lead a sedentary lifestyle, you run a high risk of osteoporosis. If you smoked heavily for many years, you may well develop emphysema. In many cases, the link between lifestyle and illness is readily apparent. With fibromyalgia, this is not the case. Nothing you did, even in your reckless youth, contributed to your fibromyalgia.

Scientists still can't pinpoint a specific cause for the syndrome that has caused so much havoc in your life. While a diagnosis sometimes follows a traumatic injury, such as one you might have sustained in a traffic accident, the injury doesn't necessarily cause the syndrome.

Even so, because no concrete cause has been found, many sufferers are convinced that they have fibromyalgia because of something they did or failed to do—not getting enough sleep perhaps, or burning the candle at both ends in their youth. Don't fall into that trap. One day there will be an identified cause and a cure for fibromyalgia. Until then, try to accept the reality of the situation and carve out a new lifestyle that accommodates your new health condition.

The challenge for you lies in accepting the fact that you have no real control over your fibromyalgia. For some people, it is not easy. But it's a necessary step in adjusting to your new life. Now, say it one more time and with conviction: "It's not my fault."

Comfort Zone

A blessing is the last idea you'd ever associate with fibromyalgia. But if you can muddle through to the other side and accept your new reality, you may find there is a silver lining. When this happens, your perspective shifts and you no longer focus on the negative changes. For instance, you know now who your true friends are; they are the ones who remained in touch, the ones who brought you meals, listened to you, even accompanied you to doctor's appointments. Maybe scaling back on your job has meant more time at home with your children. And while your energy level is too low for some activities, you've relished all the time you've spent together on the sofa, snuggling, catching up on movies, reading together.

Pain and illness is part of the human condition. In the hands of gifted writers, it can make for moving literature. While none of the following books deal specifically with fibromyalgia, each in some way covers an aspect of chronic illness, from grieving or blaming to surviving. Each is a classic in its genre.

A Grief Observed by C. S. Lewis is an honest look at grief and the process of grieving. This very intimate work was written in 1961 after the death of Lewis's beloved wife.

Illness as Metaphor by Susan Sontag. In this provocative 1973 classic, Sontag showed how the metaphors and myths surrounding certain illnesses, especially cancer, can contribute to a patient's suffering. Sontag was herself a cancer patient when she wrote it.

The Yellow Wallpaper written in 1892 by feminist and sociologist Charlotte Perkins Gilman. This classic memoir chronicles Gilman's confinement to bed—a common medical treatment back then for nervous disorders.

Helpful resources

The Chronic Illness Workbook:
Strategies and Solutions for
Taking Back Your Life
by Patricia A. Fennell,

Fibromyalgia: Simple Relief
Through Movement
by Stacie L. Bigelow

From Fatigued to Fantastic
by Jacob Teitelbaum

Guilt Is the Teacher, Love Is the
Lesson: A Book to Heal You,
Heart and Soul
by Joan Borysenko

American Chronic Pain
Association
P.O. Box 850
Rocklin, CA 95677
800-533-3231
www.theacpa.org

American Pain Society
4700 W. Lake Avenue
Glenview, IL 60025
847-375-4715
www.ampainsoc.org

National Association of
Social Workers
750 First Street NE, Suite 700
Washington, DC, 20002
Clinical social workers are the
nation's largest providers of mental
health and therapy services, out-
numbering both psychologists and
psychiatrists. They provide mental
health services in both urban and
rural settings, where they may be
the only licensed provider of mental
health services available.
202-408-8600
www.socialworkers.org

The New Normal

Life with a chronic illness
it can be a rocky road

In your not-too-distant past, whenever you got sick, you went to a doctor, got a prescription, maybe had a little surgery, felt better, and went on with your life. But fibromyalgia—despite modern medicine's best efforts—defies this pattern. Sure, there are treatments that can provide relief. But the reality is that for you now, having a chronic illness is your new-normal.

Like other major changes in your life, such as switching careers or becoming a parent, the adjustment to life as a person who has fibromyalgia can be rough. But you are not alone. So many people have chronic pain that it has become something of a national epidemic.

Actually, a diagnosis of a nonterminal illness like fibromyalgia can be a relief. After all, who wouldn't be happy to know they don't have a degenerative illness or an inoperable brain tumor? But that euphoria can be short-lived and is by no means a universal reaction to the disease called fibromyalgia. Many people are overcome with sadness. Others may become angry, and still others resigned. The emotions elicited by chronic illness are similar to the stages of grief. In fact, you are grieving over your lost health and all the ramifications of that loss.

Living with chronic illness requires an ongoing search for a positive quality of life. For those with a chronic illness there are two goals: dealing with the medical problem itself and coping with the ways that illness affects their life and lifestyle. Those who are most successful in their dealings with a chronic disease eventually find ways to tap their reserves of creativity, intelligence, and perseverance.

Remember, your diagnosis and the changes that come with it throw some big changes at your partner, too. Your other half can feel a little overwhelmed with all there is to learn. Living with a chronic illness, or with someone who has one, is challenging. And, yes, there will be frustrations.

There are several aspects of chronic illness that make it especially difficult for others to understand. One is that fibromyalgia is invisible. It's not like walking around with a broken leg. Or even coping with a life-threatening illness like cancer. People may think, "Get over yourself. You are just tired." All they will see is you retreating to your bedroom because you can't cope.

There will also be a lack of consistency in your symptoms. It's hard for people to truly understand how you can be fine for weeks at a time and then miss days of work or a social activity because you have a bad flare-up of pain. You could as be healthy as the proverbial horse in the evening and sick as a dog the next morning. That unpredictability can make both you and your family anxious. All of us are great at rallying around people in an emergency. We're not that good with painful symptoms that strike at will.

Considering all of these factors, it's not surprising that you feel that there's a lack of understanding around you. At the best of times, you need to talk about your feelings, and that's doubly true if you have a chronic illness. You need to learn to talk about the change from the old you to the new you.

The most important thing to remember is that you're not alone. There are millions of people who experience chronic pain in the U.S.; they are young and old, from all walks of life, and the majority are coping with it, leading fulfilling lives. You can, too.

Stages of adjustment
from shock to acceptance

Researchers are discovering that how people cope with the news of chronic illness has a phenomenal effect on long-term physical and emotional health. It's natural to experience what we know as the five stages of grief, defined by Dr. Elisabeth Kubler-Ross in her groundbreaking work, *On Death and Dying*. They are anger, denial, bargaining, depression, and acceptance. Take a look at these stages to see where you are. You may not encounter all of them; they are simply a blueprint of how most people respond to loss—be it of a loved one or of their health.

Denial

Once you get the diagnosis, you realize that symptoms are something you always need to be aware of. For some people, especially those with severe fibromyalgia, and even those people who have milder forms of the illness, it can be tough to make lifestyle adjustments, such as taking medication and exercising. Surprisingly, some people try to deny their suffering and just hope it goes away. What's the reason for this? For most people, it's fear. There is a loss of personal power, of self-esteem. There is also a loss of independence because your fibromyalgia inevitably interferes with how you want to manage your life. Going back to your doctor for a new treatment plan seems futile, or so you think. You opt to deny any problems. But if you're not careful, denial can become dangerous defiance. "I'll just take a vacation or some time off from work!" you might tell yourself, or: "I'll just take more ibuprofen."

What to do?

Think through the situation. What would you tell a friend who was experiencing severe muscle pain? Probably the same thing your family and friends are telling you. Seek help. Don't self-diagnose.

Anger, depression, and bargaining

You're mad at everything and everyone. "I see my doctor for checkups. I give to animal welfare groups. I am a good person. This just isn't fair!" Your friends, family, and colleagues go on as if your fibromyalgia isn't any big deal. You know you don't have a serious illness with a capital S, and you're not going to die from this thing—but you feel depressed since no one seems to understand what you are going through. You may even want to bargain your way out of fibromyalgia. "If I rest a lot and eat only organic foods, I'll get well."

What to do?

You will have to remind yourself that you'll have some great days and some not-so-great days, and there is no such thing as total recovery. Fibromyalgia is with you daily because there is no cure. One important fact to remember is that contrary to what's commonly believed, the majority of people living with chronic illnesses are not elderly or disabled. More than half are between the ages of 18 and 64, and few report they limit their activities solely based on their disease.

Acceptance

Having gone through some or all of the previous stages, you now accept your illness as part of yourself, a reality to be lived with, not escaped. You recognize that your best chance for future happiness lies in your understanding of the condition and in your disciplined commitment to its control.

Beyond acceptance
your job now is to re-create your life

Learning to accept a chronic disorder as part of your life is not easy. You miss the old carefree you. You miss not having to think about your health. You now fully understand why your grandparents used to say, "Don't take your health for granted." And you know what you have to do. With that knowledge comes a certain amount of power. It gives you back control over your life. Yes, you have this disorder, but it is treatable and it need not define who you are. You are still you, just a bit different thanks to your fibromyalgia. Yes, it is a different life than the one you had originally planned, before you got this problem, but that's okay. The point is to work with this new reality and make it your own. Here are some helpful suggestions:

Learn about your condition

Becoming a student of your condition can be an important way to know what is going on with your body. Use as many sources as you can to gather information so you understand what doctors are doing to help you. Learn about your medications and watch for their side effects. Follow doctors' instructions and keep focused on the goal—dealing with the disease. In this information age, it would seem easy to access knowledge, but be cautious. Myths about fibromyalgia can spread quickly. Family and friends can be well intentioned but often offer unsolicited advice. Decide how much contact you want with people, because with so much advice, it can feel as if you're not doing the right thing.

Take control

The most successful fibromyalgia patients are those who are active participants in their treatment. That means you can choose who will treat you and can change your doctor if you feel your fibromyalgia is not getting the attention it deserves. You can discuss how often follow-up visits may occur to see if a fibromyalgia treatment plan is working. You can ask questions. And get answers. The message is: Be involved.

Find the Right Doctor

In the beginning, it's important to find the right doctor. Don't be afraid to insist on a doctor who understands you and communicates clearly. After all, this is a person who will be helping you regain your life. You need to have a good relationship, so find someone who will collaborate with you and take an interest in you and your care.

FIRST PERSON INSIGHTS
First me, then them

I think you have to be okay with this invisibility yourself before you can expect others to accept or understand it. When my fibromyalgia was diagnosed four years ago, my two sons were very angry at first. They acted it out by fighting with each other. It was quite an adjustment for them as I made subtle changes in how much I allowed myself to be on top of every little thing in their lives, from how neatly they did their homework papers to how closely I monitored their piano practice.

Actually, it was an adjustment for all of us. Yet over time, and after plenty of discussions, everyone has come to accept this as a part of who I am, and this is how our family now functions. They know that when I am resting, they need to be quiet and not fight.

There are times when I am so tired and don't act as they would like me to act as their mom. Sometimes, we talk about the loss one feels in dealing with any illness, and they seem to get it. Overall, they manage quite well. I think it has taught them to be more compassionate people.

—Suzy M., Frederick, MD

Beginning the journey
taking it step by step

After any diagnosis, no one is certain what the final outcome will be. It's hard to live with this new, and constant, level of uncertainty and ambiguity. But how you cope and live with this can make all the difference. What seems undoable and unmanageable is doable. To combat the chaos, patients can follow a few smart strategies. One is to obtain as much information as possible. Finding out the facts can help relieve anxiety and lessen the fear of the unknown. Besides, knowledge helps the patient regain control and make informed decisions.

Identify and avoid vicious circles

For example, having high blood pressure from heart disease may make a person feel discouraged, and being discouraged may contribute to feelings of uselessness. These feelings, in turn, can contribute to a sense of fatigue, which then may increase the feeling of being useless and unhappy. This is classic vicious-cycle behavior.

Be positive

Trying to figure out new ways to enjoy old activities is fine, but if you are feeling depressed, it also helps to focus on things that you can still do well. Remember that you are a competent, unique person—with many talents and attributes that are still yours.

- ◆ Use laughter and humor to reduce stress.

- ◆ Build on the talents and activities you can still enjoy.

- ◆ Pay attention to your body. How does it feel? How is it reacting to the things you are doing right now? Plan your day accordingly.

- ◆ Learn more about yourself. What makes you tense?

Educate

Teach your family, friends, and coworkers about fibromyalgia. Talk to your family about what you need, what you expect from treatment, and what to do if those meds don't work on occasion.

◆ Stick to your goals. Your goals should not diminish because you have fibromyalgia.

Get help

Find other people who have fibromyalgia. Though friends, coworkers, and family can be sympathetic, no one knows the pain of fibromyalgia better than those who live with it. There are many support groups online, and there may be some "live" support groups in your area. Check out local hospitals to see if they offer fibromyalgia support.

Creating a new life
it's time to create a new life

If you take a good look at your life now and the life you led even a few short years ago, you are likely to see a vast difference. It's been a gradual process of cutting out some activities, curtailing work, and devoting less time to certain friends and more to others who understand or identify with you. It's a matter of resting more, doing less, and saying "no" to a lot more things. But the funny thing is, a part of you has come to accept this new life as normal.

While you'd love to be coaching your daughter's softball team, you know that the price you'd pay afterward in exhaustion and achiness is simply not worth the effort, and you're okay with that. You'll sit quietly and comfortably in the stands instead.

It may take a long time to reach this point of acceptance, of making peace with something so uncomfortable. It's a process of internalizing a difficult problem and then coming to terms with it. How you ultimately choose to approach the new life your fibromyalgia has thrust upon you—and everyone will find their own way—will determine how well you cope and even how good you feel.

Becoming an Advocate

Giving back by helping others

One of the many things having a chronic illness can do is to teach you how to accept help with grace. For many people this is the hardest lesson. Our culture thrives on independence. Those who ask for help are often chided for being lazy or inept. Another reason it's hard to ask for help is that many of us have internalized those voices of derision that say we are bad for asking. And so we don't ask, or if we do, we feel ashamed about it.

Having a chronic illness changes all that. You have no choice but to ask for help. And over time, you learn that there is nothing kinder and more loving than help freely given. Small wonder that people who have undergone great physical and emotional trials are the ones who give back to others who are suffering.

There are many ways you can give back. You can go online and add your knowledge to the various support groups on the Internet that provide so much help to those in the throes of early diagnosis (see page 93 for Web addresses). You can also join the various nonprofit organizations that support fibromyalgia research. You can volunteer to help with their newsletters and other activities. Becoming an advocate is a great way to share your illness story with others.

Helpful resources

The Chronic Illness Workbook
by Patricia A. Fennell

On Death and Dying
by Elisabeth Kubler-Ross

Recrafting a Life
by Charlie Johnson and
Denise Webster

On Being Ill
by Virginia Woolf

Illness as Metaphor
by Susan Sontag

Glossary

Acetaminophen Available over-the-counter in a number of different brands (e.g. Tylenol), this non-aspirin pain reliever is used to reduce fevers and to treat body aches, headaches and more.

Acupressure The application of pressure to specific muscle sites to relieve pain and spasms.

Acupuncture An ancient Chinese method of pain treatment that has gained popularity in the U.S. in the last few decades. Needles are inserted in areas of the body associated with pain blockage.

Alternative medicine Also known as complementary medicine, a system involving treatments and medications that are not viewed as traditional and haven't undergone rigorous scientific evaluation.

Adrenal glands Located near the kidneys, these glands secrete cortisol aldosterone, and androgens. These hormones impact blood pressure, increasing the heart and respiration rates when a person feels scared, threatened, or angry.

Antidepressants Prescription medicines that are used to lift depression or sad moods. Tricyclic antidepressants, which may relieve nighttime muscle spasms in fibromyalgia sufferers, work by increasing hormones that influence moods. A new type of antidepressants, selective serotonin reuptake inhibitors (SSRIs) such as Prozac, increase the body's levels of serotonin, a neurotransmitter that impacts mood.

Arthritis An illness that affects the joints of the body. From the Greek word: *arth* meaning joint, and "itis," meaning inflammation.

Biofeedback A procedure that uses electrical equipment to increase your awareness of your body's reaction to stress and pain and to help you to control your body's physical reactions.

Capsaicin A chemical found in some hot peppers. Capsaicin gives these peppers their "hot" sensation and does have pain-relief benefits. It is available in nonprescription creams that can be applied to achy body parts.

Chronic fatigue syndrome (CFS) A medical condition characterized by long-term fatigue and pain and often confused with fibromyalgia.

Cortisol Stress hormone that's been found in abnormal levels in some people with fibromyalgia.

Delta-wave sleep Deep, restorative sleep, in which a type of brain wave called a delta wave is produced.

Disturbances in this type of sleep are common among people with fibromyalgia.

Depression A state of mind characterized by abnormal sadness or despair. Many people with fibromyalgia are also depressed. This condition is very treatable.

Endorphins Natural painkillers produced by the nervous system that have qualities similar to opiate drugs. Endorphins are also released during exercise and laughter.

Fibromyalgia A noninfectious, chronic pain condition that is characterized by muscle pain, fatigue, nonrestorative sleep, and tender points throughout the body. It produces no abnormal X-ray or laboratory findings and is therefore difficult to diagnose. It is often associated with headaches and irritable bowel syndrome.

Fibro fog Mental confusion and forgetfulness that sometimes goes hand-in-hand with a fibro flare.

Fibrositis An out-of-date term for fibromyalgia.

Flare A casual term used to describe when the symptoms or condition are at their worst.

Gate theory A theory of how pain signals travel to the brain; pain signals, according to this theory, must travel through a pain "gate," that can be opened or closed by various positive or negative factors.

Glucocorticoids Hormones produced in your body that are related to cortisone. They can also be synthetically produced and have powerful anti-inflammatory effects.

Hypothalamus The part of your brain that regulates many of your body's vital functions, including progression through the stages of sleep.

Irritable bowel syndrome A chronic condition with symptoms that include diarrhea, constipation, and sometimes alternating bouts of each. People with fibromyalgia often have this condition.

Juvenile primary fibromyalgia Fibromyalgia in children.

Lupus (systemic lupus erythematosus) An inflammatory connective tissue autoimmune disease that can involve skin, joints, kidneys, blood, and other organs.

Metabolism Your body's continuous chemical and physical processes, which consist of building up and breaking down molecules and creating waste products.

Myalgia Pain of the muscles.

Myofascial pain syndrome A localized area of muscle and surrounding tissue pain or tenderness.

Narcotic A classification of drugs that reduce pain by blocking pain signals traveling from the central nervous system to the brain.

NSAID A nonsteroidal anti-inflammatory drug. A type of pain-relieving drug that works by reducing inflammation.

Pituitary A small gland located at the base of the brain that secretes pituitary hormones. These play a vital part in growth and development and in how the body uses and stores energy and in the activity of other glands.

Rapid eye movement sleep (REM sleep) The period of sleep in which people dream; it derives its name from the rapid eye movements that occur under closed lids during this period.

Rheumatic disease A general term to describe conditions characterized by pain and stiffness of the joints or muscles.

Serotonin A hormone that constricts blood vessels and contracts smooth muscle.

Substance P A molecule produced in the spinal cord in response to an injury to the body. Substance P stimulates nerve endings and produces pain, thereby notifying the brain of injury and danger.

Syndrome A collection of symptoms and/or physical findings that characterize a particular abnormal condition or illness.

Tender point injection Injecting a painkilling medication directly into a tender point.

Index

A

acceptance, 205
acetaminophen, 42
  dosage, 43
acupressure, 155
acupuncture, 148–149
adjustment
  of attitude, 174
  stages of, 204–205
advocate
  becoming a, 211
  finding a, 110–111
allodynia, 32
alternative practitioners, finding, 139
alternative therapies. See complementary
  therapies
"AM and PM Stretch" (video), 57
American Academy of Family Physicians, 88
American Academy of Medical Acupuncture,
  149
American Academy of Pain Medicine, 106
American Academy of Physical Medicine and
  Rehabilitation, 105
American Association of Sex Educators,
  Counselors, and Therapists, 180
American Board of Medical Specialties, 91
American Chiropractic Association, 153
American Chronic Pain Association, 62, 119,
  200
American College for the Advancement of
  Medicine, 156
American College of Rheumatology, 89, 90
American Council on Science and Health, 156
American Dietetic Association, 129, 134
  Complete Food and Nutrition Guide, 134
American Fibromyalgia Syndrome
  Association, 166
American Heart Association, 124
American Management Association, 179
American Medical Association (AMA), 90
American Pain Foundation, 60, 62
American Pain Society, 200
American Physical Therapy Association, 105
American with Disabilities Act, 184

Amitriptyline, 53
  and sleep, 55
ANA. See antinuclear antibody
analgesics, 42–43
Anaspaz, 71
anger, 205
anticonvulsants, 48, 49
antihistamines, 76
antinuclear antibody (ANA) test, 12
anxiety, 10
  long-term negative stress and, 170
Arizona State University, 159
Arthritis Foundation, 26, 62, 89, 192
  on juvenile fibromyalgia, 72
Aspercreme, 44
aspirin, 42
  dosage, 43
Association for Applied Psychophysiology &
  Biofeedback, 143
attitude adjustments, 174

B

baths
  hot, for fibromyalgia, 22
  warm, for irritable bowel syndrome, 71
Beehive, The, 91
Ben Gay, 44
Benson, Herbert, 144
Bentyl, 71
Bigelow, Stacie, 56
binge eating, 172
biofeedback, 142–143
Biofeedback Certification of America, 143
Bitartrate with acetaminophen, 51
blood tests, 12–13
body imaging tests, 13
bodywork, 154–155
books
  after diagnosis, 96
  alternative therapies, 156
  on chronic fatigue syndrome, 72
  on chronic illness, 26, 200
  on chronic muscle pain, 38

M

magnesium, 146

magnetic resonance imaging (MRI), 13

malic acid, 146

massage, 22, 154, 178

  Swedish massage, 155

Mayo Clinic, 88–89, 159

McGill University, 160

McGrath, Patrick, 79

medications

  anticonvulsants, 48, 49

  clinical trials, 164–165

  generic, 109

  for irritable bowel syndrome, 71

  keeping list of, 108

  narcotics, 50–51

  new, 160

  over-the counter, 42–43

  pain medications log, 112

  personalized prescriptions, 160

  prescription, 48–49

  for sleep dysfunction, 54–55

  topical creams, 44

Medi-Net, 91

meditation, 144–145, 178

MedLine, 88

memory loss, stress and, 172

menthol, 44

metabolism, 123

methyl salicylate, 44

mind/body issues, 137

Mineral Ice, 44

minerals, 146–147

Mirapex, 160

MRI. See magnetic resonance imaging

mucous colitis. See irritable bowel syndrome (IBS)

muscle relaxants

  and myofascial pain syndrome, 66

  and sleep, 55

muscles

  chronic muscle tension, 172

  progressive muscle relaxation, 140

myofascial pain syndrome, 66–67

myofascial therapy, 155

N

narcotics, 50–51

National Association of Cognitive-Behavioral Therapists, 59, 62

National Association of Social Workers, 116, 120, 200

National Center for Complementary and Alternative Medicine (NCCAM), 138, 139, 156

National Certification Board for Therapeutic Massage and Bodywork, 154

National Certification Commission for Acupuncture and Oriental Medicine, 149

National Fibromyalgia Association, 82, 166

National Foundation for the Treatment of Pain, 87

National Institute of Arthritis and Musculoskeletal and Skin Diseases, 26

  clinical studies, 158

National Institutes of Health, 88

  on acupuncture, 148

  on biofeedback, 142

National Library of Medicine, 88, 139, 166

National Mental Health Association, 91, 120

National Qigong Association, 151

NCCAM. See National Center for Complementary and Alternative Medicine

negativity

  in coping responses, 171

  managing, 190–191

  and pain, 22

nerve conduction testing, 13

Neurology, 162

Neurontin, 48, 49

new life, creating a, 210

newsgroups, 94–95

  alt.support.fibromyalgia, 94

norepinephrine, 169

normal life, leading a, 201–212

Nortriptyline, 53

220